Ninja Air Fryer
Cookbook for Beginners

Simple & Delicious Ninja Air Fryer Recipes for Your Family & Friends

Julia Adamo

TABLE OF CONTENTS

Chapter 1-Introduction 5
- What is Ninja Air Fryer Max XL? 6
- Benefits of the Ninja Air Fryer Max XL 6
- Main Functions of Ninja Air Fryer Max XL 6
- Buttons and User Guide of Ninja Air Fryer Max XL 7
- Cleaning and Maintenance of Ninja Air Fryer Max XL 7

Chapter 2-Breakfast Recipes 8
- Cinnamon Toasts 8
- Egg and Avocado in The Ninja Foodi 8
- Breakfast Sausage Omelet 9
- Bacon and Egg Omelet 9
- Sweet Potatoes Hash 10
- Bacon and Eggs for Breakfast 10
- Yellow Potatoes with Eggs 11
- Pumpkin Muffins 11
- Egg with Baby Spinach 12
- Air Fried Sausage 12
- Morning Egg Rolls 13
- Pepper Egg Cups 13
- Spinach Egg Muffins 14
- Morning Patties 14
- Breakfast Casserole 15
- Crispy Hash Browns 15
- Banana and Raisins Muffins 16
- Sausage with Eggs 16
- Biscuit Balls 17
- Breakfast Bacon 17

Chapter 3-Snacks and Appetizers Recipes 18
- Crispy Tortilla Chips 18
- Chicken Crescent Wraps 18
- Strawberries and Walnuts Muffins 19
- Fried Halloumi Cheese 19
- Stuffed Bell Peppers 20
- Sweet Bites 20
- Spicy Chicken Tenders 21
- Grill Cheese Sandwich 21
- Parmesan Crush Chicken 22
- Dijon Cheese Sandwich 22
- Onion Rings 23
- Peppered Asparagus 23
- Chicken Tenders 24
- Crispy Plantain Chips 24
- Cauliflower Gnocchi 25
- Parmesan French Fries 25
- Blueberries Muffins 26
- Cheddar Quiche 26
- Potato Tater Tots 27
- Chicken Stuffed Mushrooms 28

Chapter 4-Beef, Lamb and Pork Recipes 29
- Ham Burger Patties 29
- Spicy Lamb Chops 29
- Short Ribs & Root Vegetables 30
- Bell Peppers with Sausages 30
- Chinese BBQ Pork 31
- Glazed Steak Recipe 31
- Steak and Mashed Creamy Potatoes 32
- Steak in Air Fry 32
- Beef & Broccoli 33
- Pork Chops 33
- Yogurt Lamb Chops 34
- Beef Ribs I 34
- Beef Ribs II 35
- Chipotle Beef 35
- Zucchini Pork Skewers 36
- Mustard Rubbed Lamb Chops 36
- Air Fryer Meatloaves 37
- Lamb Shank with Mushroom Sauce 37
- Parmesan Pork Chops 38
- Pork Chops with Broccoli 38
- Turkey and Beef Meatballs 39
- Pork with Green Beans and Potatoes 40
- Gochujang Brisket 40
- Beef Cheeseburgers 41
- Pork Chops with Brussels Sprouts 42

Chapter 5-Chicken and Poultry Recipes . 43
- Glazed Thighs with French Fries 43
- Balsamic Duck Breast 43
- Sweet and Spicy Carrots with Chicken Thighs 44
- Wings with Corn on Cob 44
- Yummy Chicken Breasts 45
- Chicken Thighs with Brussels sprouts 45
- Chicken & Broccoli 46
- Chicken Leg Piece 46
- Spiced Chicken and Vegetables 47
- Cornish Hen with Baked Potatoes 47
- Chicken Breast Strips 48
- Cornish Hen with Asparagus 48

Spicy Chicken 49
Spice-Rubbed Chicken Pieces 49
Chicken Wings 50
Crumbed Chicken Katsu 50
Pickled Chicken Fillets 51
Crusted Chicken Breast 51
Chicken Potatoes 52
Chicken Drumettes 52
Chili Chicken Wings 53
Brazilian Chicken Drumsticks 54
Bang-Bang Chicken 54
Veggie Stuffed Chicken Breasts 55
General Tso's Chicken 55
Bacon-Wrapped Chicken 56
Air Fried Turkey Breast 57
Cheddar-Stuffed Chicken 57

Chapter 6-Seafood and Fish Recipes 58

Seafood Shrimp Omelet 58
Salmon with Broccoli and Cheese 58
Salmon with Green Beans 59
Fish and Chips 59
Codfish with Herb Vinaigrette 60
Spicy Fish Fillet with Onion Rings 60
Beer Battered Fish Fillet 61
Keto Baked Salmon with Pesto 61
Smoked Salmon 62
Two-Way Salmon 62
Lemon Pepper Salmon with Asparagus 63
Salmon with Coconut 63
Frozen Breaded Fish Fillet 64
Salmon Nuggets 64
Fish Sandwich 65
Breaded Scallops 65
Salmon Patties 66
Glazed Scallops 66
Salmon with Fennel Salad 67
Crusted Tilapia 67
Scallops with Greens 68
Crusted Cod 68
Crusted Shrimp 69
Crispy Catfish 69
Savory Salmon Fillets 70
Fried Lobster Tails 70
Buttered Mahi-Mahi 71

Chapter 7-Vegetables Recipes 72

Stuffed Tomatoes 72
Saucy Carrots 72
Zucchini with Stuffing 73
Green Beans with Baked Potatoes 73
Cheesy Potatoes with Asparagus 74
Kale and Spinach Chips 74
Mixed Air Fry Veggies 75
Garlic Herbed Baked Potatoes 75
Garlic Potato Wedges in Air Fryer 76
Fresh Mix Veggies in Air Fryer 76
Brussels Sprouts 77
Curly Fries 77
Falafel 78
Fried Artichoke Hearts 78
Lime Glazed Tofu 79
Sweet Potatoes with Honey Butter 79
Zucchini Cakes 80
Hasselback Potatoes 80
Air Fried Okra 81
Fried Olives 81
Quinoa Patties 82

Chapter 8-Desserts Recipes 83

Cake in the Air Fryer 83
Bread Pudding 83
Tasty Pumpkin Muffins 84
Air Fryer Sweet Twists 84
Mini Strawberry and Cream Pies 85
Lemony Sweet Twists 85
Chocolate Chip Muffins 86
Chocolate Chip Cake 86
Mini Blueberry Pies 87
Apple Hand Pies 87
Apple Nutmeg Flautas 88
Air Fried Beignets 88
Air Fried Bananas 89
Apple Crisp 89
Zesty Cranberry Scones 90
Walnuts Fritters 90
Oreo Rolls 91
Biscuit Doughnuts 91
Fudge Brownies 92

Chapter 9-4 Weeks Diet Plan 93

Week-1 93
Week-2 93
Week-3 94
Week-4 94

Conclusion 95

Appendix Measurement Conversion Chart
.... 96

Chapter 1-Introduction

People are too busy in their life to have time for cooking food for a long time in their kitchen. They want to eat delicious and healthy food with less time. The Ninja Air Fryer Max XL solves your problem because it will give you healthy, quick, and delicious food with less time. If you are worried about food flavor and texture, there is no need to worry about it. "The Ninja Air Fryer Max XL" gives you delicious food without changing its taste and texture. The Ninja Air Fryer Max XL is unique because it can fry, roast, bake, dehydrate, max crisp, broil, and reheat your food.

You can prepare restaurant-style food at home in your Ninja Air Fryer Max XL without any hesitation. After reading this book, you will understand all features of this appliance. The Ninja Air Fryer Max XL takes air frying to next level with the highest temperature 450 degrees Fahrenheit in max crisp cooking function. The temperature is perfect when cooking frozen foods. You can prepare crispy chicken breast from frozen chicken, and you can prepare chicken patties, French fries, and breaded shrimp; this appliance makes them crispy and delicious when cooked on this max crisp setting.

Seven programmable functions in the Ninja Air Fryer Max XL means you don't need a different appliance for baking, dehydrating, roasting, broiling, and reheating food. Adjust temperature and time for making foods such as pork, beef, lamb, fish, chicken, vegetables, etc. Just press the button according to the recipe's guidance.

The larger-capacity basket that comes with the Ninja Air Fryer Max XL allows you to cook a large portion of food simultaneously. You don't need to cook food in batches as you do with other air fryers. In the Ninja Air Fryer Max XL, your food will be delicious, tender, juicy, and healthy with even less time.

The best thing is that the cleaning method is simple. When the air fryer is cooled completely, wipe down the inside and outside with a cloth. The accessories of the air fryer can go right into the dishwasher. It takes less time to clean than utensils. You can relax and enjoy yourself with your family instead of being tired in your kitchen. You don't need to stand for a long time in your kitchen. You will find delicious recipes from this book. If you have Ninja Air Fryer Max XL on your counter, you can make recipes that are delicious for your health.

Why Ninja Air Fryer Max XL? It has ample capacity to cook food, seven useful cooking features, and high temperature. All these ensure you get perfect results every time.

With these seven programmable cooking appliances, you can prepare your favorite food on any occasion. So, let's start cooking with "the Ninja Air Fryer Max XL.

What is Ninja Air Fryer Max XL?

The Ninja Air Fryer Max XL has accessories like racks, a crisper plate, and an air fryer basket made with ceramic coating. You can make food with seven different cooking functions: max crisp, air broil, air roast, bake, reheat, dehydrate, and air fry. It has max-crisp technology. With this function, you can prepare frozen food (without thawing) in less time. This cooking appliance is easy to clean. If you want the best results, remove food immediately after complete cooking time to avoid overcooking. You don't need to adjust the temperature for max crisp cooking function because it takes the hottest temperature 450 degrees Fahrenheit. For more details, read this book thoroughly.

Benefits of the Ninja Air Fryer Max XL

MAX CRISP Technology
The Ninja Air Fryer Max XL has been developed to cook frozen foods. Now, you don't thaw frozen food for many hours. You can prepare frozen food directly into this kitchen appliance. Press the "MAX CRISP" button and prepare chicken nuggets, French fries, breaded shrimp. Cook frozen foods and make them extra crisp and crunch in little-to-no oil with MAX CRISP cooking function.

Seven-in-One Program
The 7-in-1 programs on the Ninja Air Fryer Max XL include max crisp, air fry, air roast, air broil, bake, reheat, and dehydrate. You can adjust the cooking temperature for all these functions except max crisp, which heats at 450 degrees Fahrenheit. Now, you can select your favorite cooking function and prepare food for your family and friends.

Fast Cooking of Frozen Foods
When you place frozen veggies or frozen meat into the air fryer, they will be hot and tender in ten to fifteen minutes.

Easy to Clean
The best part of the Ninja Air Fryer Max XL is simple to clean. Firstly, unplug the air fryer, wait for it to cool down, remove the accessories from the unit, put them into the dishwasher, or clean it with a non-abrasive sponge or soapy water. The air fryer basket and racks are prepared with non-stick coating, and they are easy to clean. Wipe down the inside and outside of the unit with a damp cloth.

Main Functions of Ninja Air Fryer Max XL

These seven cooking functions are unique on The Ninja Air Fryer Max XL. All you need to do is press your favorite function, and the unit will cook different foods perfectly. You need to adjust the cooking time and temperature.

Max Crisp
The Ninja Air Fryer Max XL has a new cooking feature, "MAX CRISP." You didn't need to adjust the temperature because it is already adjusted at the highest temperature, 450 degrees Fahrenheit. This cooking function is designed for frozen food. It gives frozen food crispy, brown, and

delicious flavor and texture. Prepare French fries, chicken nuggets, and shrimp with little to no oil.

Air Fry
This cooking function is used for deep-frying cooking. Using this function, you will get crispy and tender fried food. This function also needs little to no oil for cooking foods. The fan speed of this appliance is more powerful than other appliances. You can open the basket and check the food without any afraid.

Air Broil
Broiling is a great way to cook steaks or salmon fillets. This function is used to finish the recipe. If food is cooked well and you want it to have browned crust, place the food back to the basket, insert it into the air fryer, and press the air broil button. Within just a minute, you will have perfect crispy and browned food.

Dehydrate
Dehydrating foods is a great way to preserve them. The cooking function uses low heat and a fan to remove the moisture from the food. You can prepare tender, juicy, and delicious chips from spinach, beetroot, bananas, apples, kale, sweet potatoes, and mangoes with the dehydrated cooking function. But, the dehydrating cooking function needs a lot of time to prepare food. Using this function, you can dehydrate the food overnight while you sleep to be ready in the morning. For best results, dry the food and trim fat from the food before dehydrating them.

Air Roast
Air roast cooking function needs high heat to cook food. It cooks the inner part of the meat. You can roast food in less time. Air roasted food is juicy and tender on the inside, with incredible texture and flavor.

Bake
Baking is one of my favorite cooking functions. With this function, you can bake cakes, muffins, cupcakes, brownies, pancakes, and puddings, etc. You don't need to purchase another appliance for baking foods. Adjust the time and temperature for baking food.

Reheat
Reheat is the best option for leftover food. If you have leftover food, you don't need to put it onto the stovetop; otherwise, it loses its taste. With the reheat function, you will get food with the same texture and flavor.

Buttons and User Guide of Ninja Air Fryer Max XL

The method of Ninja Air Fryer Max XL is pretty simple. It has four operating buttons.

TEMP arrows
Pressing the TEMP arrows, you can adjust the temperature according to the recipe's instructions. You can adjust the temperature for all functions except max crisp.

TIME arrows
Pressing the TIME arrows, you can adjust the time according to the recipe's instructions. You can adjust the time for all cooking functions.

START/STOP button
When you select the time and temperature, press the start/stop button and stop the cooking after pressing this button again.

POWER button
When you press the power button, the unit will turn off and stops all cooking progress.

Cleaning and Maintenance of Ninja Air Fryer Max XL

Cleaning and maintenance of this appliance are pretty easy.
- Unplug the unit from the wall outlet before cleaning and allow the unit to cool. Remove all accessories from the unit and cool them down.
- Never immerse the main unit into the water or any other liquid.
- Wipe the main unit and control panel with a damp cloth.
- Remove the crisper plate, basket, and other accessories from the unit and put them into the dishwasher.
- If food is stuck onto the basket or crisper basket, put it into the lightly warm soapy water.
- When all parts get dried, return to the unit.

Chapter 2-Breakfast Recipes

Cinnamon Toasts

Prep Time: 15 minutes.
Cook Time: 8 minutes.
Serves: 4
Ingredients:
- 4 pieces of bread
- 2 tablespoons butter
- 2 eggs, beaten
- 1 pinch salt
- 1 pinch cinnamon ground
- 1 pinch nutmeg ground
- 1 pinch ground clove
- 1 teaspoon icing sugar

Preparation:
1. At 390 degrees F, preheat your Air Fryer on Air Fry mode.
2. Add two eggs to a mixing bowl and stir cinnamon, nutmeg, ground cloves, and salt, then whisk well.
3. Spread butter on both sides of the bread slices and cut them into thick strips.
4. Dip the breadsticks in the egg mixture and place them in the Air Fryer Basket.
5. Return the Air Fryer Basket to the Air Fryer and cook for 8 minutes.
6. Initiate cooking by pressing the START/PAUSE BUTTON.
7. Flip the French toast sticks when cooked halfway through.
8. Serve.

Serving Suggestion: Serve the toasted with chocolate syrup or Nutella spread.
Variation Tip: Use crushed cornflakes for breading to have extra crispiness.
Nutritional Information Per Serving:
Calories 199 | Fat 11.1g | Sodium 297mg | Carbs 14.9g | Fiber 1g | Sugar 2.5g | Protein 9.9g

Egg and Avocado in The Ninja Foodi

Prep Time: 10 Minutes
Cook Time: 10 Minutes
Serves: 2
Ingredients
- 2 avocados, pitted and cut in half
- Garlic salt, to taste
- Cooking for greasing
- 4 eggs
- ¼ teaspoon Paprika powder, for sprinkling
- ⅓ cup parmesan cheese, crumbled
- 6 bacon strips, raw

Directions
1. Preheat the unit by selecting AIR FRY mode for 3 minutes at 325 degrees F.
2. Select START/PAUSE to begin the preheating process.
3. Next, cut the avocado in half and pit it.
4. Now scoop out the flesh from the avocado and keep intact some of it.
5. Crack one egg in each hole of avocado and sprinkle paprika and garlic salt
6. Top it with cheese at the end.
7. Now pour it into tin foil and then put it in the air fryer basket along with bacon strips.
8. Set it to AIR FRY mode at 400 degrees F for 10 minutes.
9. Press START/PAUSE to initiate cooking.
10. Once done, serve and enjoy.

Serving Suggestion: Serve it with Bread slices.
Variation Tip: Use butter for greasing.
Nutritional Information Per Serving: Calories 609 | Fat 53.2g | Sodium 335mg | Carbs 18.1g | Fiber 13.5g | Sugar 1.7g | Protein 21.3g

Breakfast Sausage Omelet

Prep Time: 10 Minutes
Cook Time: 15 Minutes
Serves: 2
Ingredients
- ¼ pound breakfast sausage, cooked and crumbled
- 4 eggs, beaten
- ½ cup pepper Jack cheese blend
- 2 tablespoons green bell pepper, sliced
- 1 green onion, chopped
- 1 pinch cayenne pepper
- Cooking spray

Directions
1. Take a bowl and whisk eggs in it along with crumbled sausage, pepper Jack cheese, green onions, red bell pepper, and cayenne pepper.
2. Mix it all well.
3. Take cake pan that fit inside the Ninja air fryer and grease it with oil spray.
4. Pour the omelet mixture into the cake pan.
5. Preheat the unit by selecting AIR FRY mode for 3 minutes at 325 degrees F.
6. Select START/PAUSE to begin the preheating process.
7. Once preheating is done, put the cake pan inside the basket and place the basket inside the unit.
8. Turn on the Air Fry function and let it cook for 15-20 minutes at 310 degrees F.
9. Once the cooking cycle completes, take out, and serve hot, as a delicious breakfast.
Serving Suggestion: Serve it with ketchup.
Variation Tip: Use Parmesan cheese instead of pepper jack Cheese.
Nutritional Information Per Serving: Calories 691| Fat 52.4g | Sodium1122 mg | Carbs 13.3g | Fiber 1.8g| Sugar 7g | Protein 42g

Bacon and Egg Omelet

Prep Time: 12 Minutes
Cook Time: 10 Minutes
Serves: 2
Ingredients
- 2 eggs, whisked
- ½ teaspoon chopped tomatoes
- Sea Salt and black pepper, to taste
- 2 teaspoons almond milk
- 1 teaspoon cilantro, chopped
- 1 small green chili, chopped
- 4 slices bacon

Directions
1. Take a bowl and whisk eggs in it.
2. Then add green chili, salt, black pepper, cilantro, almond milk, and chopped tomatoes.
3. Oil greases two ramekins.
4. Pour this into ramekins.
5. Preheat the unit by selecting AIR FRY mode for 4 minutes at 325 degrees F.
6. Select START/PAUSE to begin the preheating process.
7. Once preheating is done, put the ramekins inside the unit along with bacon slices.
8. Set it to AIR FRY mode at 400 degrees F, for 10 minutes
9. Once 7 minutes pass, take out the basket and remove the bacon from the unit.
10. Again press START/PAUSE to finish the cooking time.
11. Once done take out the eggs from the ramekins and serve with bacons strip.
12. Enjoy hot.
Serving Suggestion: Serve it with bread slices and ketchup.
Variation Tip: Use garlic salt instead of sea salt.
Nutritional Information Per Serving: Calories 285| Fat 21.5g| Sodium1000 mg | Carbs 2.2g | Fiber 0.1g| Sugar1 g | Protein 19.7g

Sweet Potatoes Hash

Prep Time: 15 Minutes
Cook Time: 25 Minutes
Serves: 2
Ingredients
- 450 grams sweet potatoes
- ½ white onion, diced
- 3 tablespoons olive oil
- 1 teaspoon smoked paprika
- ¼ teaspoon cumin
- ⅓ teaspoon ground turmeric
- ¼ teaspoon garlic salt
- 1 cup guacamole

Directions
1. Preheat the unit by selecting AIR FRY mode for 3 minutes at 325 degrees F.
2. Select START/PAUSE to begin the preheating process.
3. Once preheating is done, press START/PAUSE.
4. Peel and cut the potatoes into cubes.
5. Now, transfer the potatoes to a bowl and add oil, white onions, cumin, paprika, turmeric, and garlic salt.
6. Put this mixture into the basket of the Ninja Foodi Air Fryer.
7. Set it to AIR FRY mode for 10 minutes at 390 degrees F.
8. Then take out the basket and shake them well.
9. Then again set time to 15 minutes at 390 degrees F.
10. Once done, serve it with guacamole.

Serving Suggestion: Serve it with ketchup and omelet.
Variation Tip: Use canola oil instead of olive oil.
Nutritional Information Per Serving: Calories691 | Fat 49.7g| Sodium 596mg | Carbs 64g | Fiber15g | Sugar 19g | Protein 8.1g

Bacon and Eggs for Breakfast

Prep Time: 12 Minutes
Cook Time: 12 Minutes
Serves: 1
Ingredients
- 4 strips thick-sliced bacon
- 2 small eggs
- Salt and black pepper, to taste
- Oil spray for greasing ramekins

Directions
1. Take 2 ramekins and grease them with oil spray.
2. Crack eggs in a bowl and season it salt and black pepper.
3. Divide the egg mixture between two ramekins.
4. Preheat the unit by selecting AIR FRY mode for 3 minutes at 325 degrees F.
5. Select START/PAUSE to begin the preheating process.
6. Once preheating is done, put the ramekin inside the bottom of the air fryer basket, and bacon on side.
7. Put the basket inside the unit.
8. Now set it to AIR FRY mode at 400 degrees F, for 12 minutes.
9. Press start to begin the cooking.
10. Once done, serve and enjoy.

Serving Suggestion: None
Variation Tip: Use butter for greasing ramekins.
Nutritional Information Per Serving: Calories131 | Fat 10g| Sodium 187mg | Carbs0.6 g | Fiber 0g | Sugar 0.6g | Protein 10.7

Yellow Potatoes with Eggs

Prep Time: 10 Minutes
Cook Time: 30 Minutes
Serves: 2

Ingredients
- 1 pound Dutch yellow potatoes, quartered
- 1 red bell pepper, chopped
- Salt and black pepper, to taste
- 1 green bell pepper, chopped
- 2 teaspoons olive oil
- 2 teaspoons garlic powder
- 1 teaspoon onion powder
- 1 egg
- ¼ teaspoon butter

Directions
1. Preheat the unit by selecting AIR FRY mode for 5 minutes at 325 degrees F.
2. Select START/PAUSE to begin the preheating process.
3. Toss together diced potatoes, green pepper, red pepper, salt, black pepper, and olive oil along with garlic powder and onion powder.
4. Take ramekin and grease it with oil spray.
5. Whisk egg in a bowl and add salt and pepper along with ½ teaspoon of butter.
6. Pour egg into a ramekin and place ramekins inside the air fryer.
7. Transfer bowl ingredients to the air fryer basket aside the ramekins.
8. Set the timer for basket to 30 minutes at 400 degrees F, on the AIR FRY mode.
9. Once preheating is done, press START/PAUSE.
10. Once 10 minutes pass, press START/PAUSE and takeout the ramekin.
11. Press the START/PAUSE button, and let the potato cook for remaining minutes.
12. Once done, serve and enjoy.

Serving Suggestion: Serve it with sourdough toasted bread slices.

Variation Tip: Use white potatoes instead of yellow Dutch potatoes.

Nutritional Information Per Serving: Calories 252 | Fat 7.5g | Sodium 37mg | Carbs 40g | Fiber 3.9g | Sugar 7g | Protein 6.7g

Pumpkin Muffins

Prep Time: 15 minutes.
Cook Time: 13 minutes.
Serves: 8

Ingredients:
- ½ cup pumpkin puree
- 1 cup gluten-free oats
- ¼ cup honey
- 1 medium egg beaten
- ½ teaspoon coconut butter
- ½ tablespoons cocoa nib
- ½ tablespoons vanilla essence
- Cooking spray
- ½ teaspoon nutmeg

Preparation:
1. At 375 degrees F, preheat your Air Fryer on Air Fry mode.
2. Add oats, honey, eggs, pumpkin puree, coconut butter, cocoa nibs, vanilla essence, and nutmeg to a bowl and mix well until smooth.
3. Divide the batter into the muffin tray, greased with cooking spray.
4. Place the muffin tray in the Air Fryer Basket.
5. Return the Air Fryer Basket to the Air Fryer and cook for 13 minutes.
6. Initiate cooking by pressing the START/PAUSE BUTTON.
7. Allow the muffins to cool, then serve.

Serving Suggestion: Serve the muffins with hot coffee.

Variation Tip: Add raisins and nuts to the batter before baking.

Nutritional Information Per Serving:
Calories 209 | Fat 7.5g | Sodium 321mg | Carbs 34.1g | Fiber 4g | Sugar 3.8g | Protein 4.3g

Egg with Baby Spinach

Prep Time: 12 Minutes
Cook Time: 12 Minutes
Serves: 4

Ingredients
- Nonstick spray, for greasing ramekins
- 2 tablespoons olive oil
- 6 ounces baby spinach
- 2 garlic cloves, minced
- ⅓ teaspoon kosher salt
- 6-8 large eggs
- ½ cup half and half
- Salt and black pepper, to taste
- 8 Sourdough bread slices, toasted

Directions
1. Preheat the unit by selecting AIR FRY mode for 2 minutes at 350 degrees F.
2. Select START/PAUSE to begin the preheating process.
3. Once preheating is done, press START/PAUSE.
4. Grease 4 ramekins with oil spray and set aside for further use.
5. Take a skillet and heat oil in it.
6. Then cook spinach for 2 minutes and add garlic and salt black pepper.
7. Let it simmer for 2 more minutes.
8. Once the spinach is wilted, transfer it to a plate.
9. Whisk an egg into a small bowl.
10. Add in the spinach.
11. Whisk it well and then pour half and half.
12. Divide this mixture between 4 ramekins and remember not to overfill it to the top, leave a little space on top.
13. Put the ramekins in the basket of the Ninja Foodi Air Fryer.
14. Select AIR FRY mode at 350 degrees F for 12 minutes. Press START/PAUSE to initiate cooking.
15. Once it's cooked and eggs are done, serve with sourdough bread slices.

Serving Suggestion: Serve it with cream cheese topping.
Variation Tip: Use plain bread slices instead of sourdough bread slices.
Nutritional Information Per Serving: Calories 404| Fat 19.6g| Sodium 761mg | Carbs 40.1g | Fiber 2.5g| Sugar 2.5g | Protein 19.2g

Air Fried Sausage

Prep Time: 10 minutes.
Cook Time: 13 minutes.
Serves: 4

Ingredients:
- 4 sausage links, raw and uncooked

Preparation:
1. At 390 degrees F, preheat your Air Fryer on Air Fry mode.
2. Place the sausages in the Air Fryer Basket.
3. Return the Air Fryer Basket to the Air Fryer and cook for 13 minutes.
4. Initiate cooking by pressing the START/PAUSE BUTTON.
5. Serve warm and fresh.

Serving Suggestion: Serve the sausages with toasted bread and eggs.
Variation Tip: Add black pepper and salt for seasoning.
Nutritional Information Per Serving:
Calories 267 | Fat 12g |Sodium 165mg | Carbs 39g | Fiber 1.4g | Sugar 22g | Protein 3.3g

Morning Egg Rolls

Prep Time: 15 minutes.
Cook Time: 13 minutes.
Serves: 6
Ingredients:
- 2 eggs
- 2 tablespoons milk
- Salt, to taste
- Black pepper, to taste
- ½ cup shredded cheddar cheese
- 2 sausage patties
- 6 egg roll wrappers
- 1 tablespoon olive oil
- 1 cup of water

Preparation:
1. At 375 degrees F, preheat your Air Fryer on Air Fry mode.
2. Grease a small skillet with some olive oil and place it over medium heat.
3. Add sausage patties and cook them until brown.
4. Chop the cooked patties into small pieces. Beat eggs with salt, black pepper, and milk in a mixing bowl.
5. Grease the same skillet with 1 teaspoon of olive oil and pour the egg mixture into it.
6. Stir cook to make scrambled eggs.
7. Add sausage, mix well and remove the skillet from the heat.
8. Spread an egg roll wrapper on the working surface in a diamond shape position.
9. Add a tablespoon of cheese at the bottom third of the roll wrapper.
10. Top the cheese with an egg mixture and wet the edges of the wrapper with water.
11. Fold the two corners of the wrapper and roll it, then seal the edges.
12. Repeat the same steps and place the rolls in the Air Fryer Basket.
13. Return the Air Fryer Basket to the Air Fryer and cook for 13 minutes.
14. Initiate cooking by pressing the START/PAUSE BUTTON.
15. Flip the rolls after 8 minutes and continue cooking for another 5 minutes.
16. Serve warm and fresh.

Serving Suggestion: Serve the rolls with your favorite hot sauce or cheese dip.
Variation Tip: Add crispy bacon to the filling.
Nutritional Information Per Serving:
Calories 282 | Fat 15g | Sodium 526mg | Carbs 20g | Fiber 0.6g | Sugar 3.3g | Protein 16g

Pepper Egg Cups

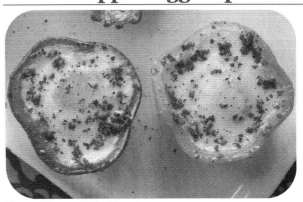

Prep Time: 15 minutes.
Cook Time: 18 minutes.
Serves: 4
Ingredients:
- 2 bell pepper, halved, seeds removed
- 4 eggs
- 1 teaspoon olive oil
- 1 pinch salt and black pepper
- 1 pinch sriracha flakes

Preparation:
1. At 390 degrees F, preheat your Air Fryer on Air Fry mode.
2. Slice the bell peppers in half, lengthwise, and remove their seeds and the inner portion to get a cup-like shape.
3. Rub olive oil on the edges of the bell peppers.
4. Place them in the Air Fryer Basket with their cut side up and crack 1 egg in each half of bell pepper.
5. Drizzle salt, black pepper, and sriracha flakes on top of the eggs.
6. Return the Air Fryer Basket to the Air Fryer and cook for 18 minutes.
7. Initiate cooking by pressing the START/PAUSE BUTTON.
8. Serve warm and fresh.

Serving Suggestion: Serve the cups with toasted bread slices and crispy bacon.
Variation Tip: Broil the cups with mozzarella cheese on top.
Nutritional Information Per Serving:
Calories 183 | Fat 15g | Sodium 402mg | Carbs 2.5g | Fiber 0.4g | Sugar 1.1g | Protein 10g

Spinach Egg Muffins

Prep Time: 10 minutes.
Cook Time: 13 minutes.
Serves: 4
Ingredients:
- 4 tablespoons milk
- 4 tablespoons frozen spinach, thawed
- 4 large egg
- 8 teaspoons grated cheese
- Salt, to taste
- Black pepper, to taste
- Cooking Spray

Preparation:
1. At 390 degrees F, preheat your Air Fryer on Air Fry mode.
2. Grease four small-sized ramekin with cooking spray.
3. Add egg, cheese, spinach, and milk to a bowl and beat well.
4. Divide the mixture into the four small ramekins and top them with salt and black pepper.
5. Place the ramekins in the Air Fryer Basket.
6. Return the Air Fryer Basket to the Air Fryer and cook for 13 minutes.
7. Initiate cooking by pressing the START/PAUSE BUTTON.
8. Serve warm.

Serving Suggestion: Serve the muffins with toasted bread slices and crispy bacon.
Variation Tip: Add sliced bell peppers to the muffins.
Nutritional Information Per Serving:
Calories 237 | Fat 19g |Sodium 518mg | Carbs 7g | Fiber 1.5g | Sugar 3.4g | Protein 12g

Morning Patties

Prep Time: 15 minutes.
Cook Time: 13 minutes.
Serves: 4
Ingredients:
- 1 lb. minced pork
- 1 lb. minced turkey
- 2 teaspoons dry rubbed sage
- 2 teaspoons fennel seeds
- 2 teaspoons garlic powder
- 1 teaspoon paprika
- 1 teaspoon sea salt
- 1 teaspoon dried thyme

Preparation:
1. At 390 degrees F, preheat your Air Fryer on Air Fry mode.
2. In a mixing bowl, add turkey and pork, then mix them together.
3. Mix sage, fennel, paprika, salt, thyme, and garlic powder in a small bowl.
4. Drizzle this mixture over the meat mixture and mix well.
5. Take 2 tablespoons of this mixture at a time and roll it into thick patties.
6. Place the patties in the Air Fryer Basket, then spray them all with cooking oil.
7. Return the Air Fryer Basket to the Air Fryer and cook for 10 minutes.
8. Initiate cooking by pressing the START/PAUSE BUTTON.
9. Flip the patties in the basket once cooked halfway through.
10. Serve warm and fresh.

Serving Suggestion: Serve the patties with toasted bread slices.
Variation Tip: Ground chicken or beef can also be used instead of ground pork and turkey.
Nutritional Information Per Serving:
Calories 305 | Fat 25g |Sodium 532mg | Carbs 2.3g | Fiber 0.4g | Sugar 2g | Protein 18.3g

Breakfast Casserole

Prep Time: 5 Minutes
Cook Time: 10 Minutes
Serves: 4

Ingredients
- 1 pound beef sausage, grounded
- ¼ cup diced white onion
- 1 diced green bell pepper
- 8 whole eggs, beaten
- ½ cup Colby jack cheese, shredded
- ¼ teaspoon garlic salt
- Oil spray, for greasing

Directions
1. Take a bowl and add ground sausage to it.
2. Add in the diced onions, bell peppers, eggs and whisk it well.
3. Then season it with garlic salt.
4. Spray the basket of the air fryer with oil spray.
5. Preheat the unit by selecting AIR FRY mode for 5 minutes at 325 degrees F.
6. Select START/PAUSE to begin the preheating process.
7. Once preheating is done, place the mixture inside the basket; remember to remove the crisper plate.
8. Top the mixture with cheese.
9. Now, turn ON the Ninja Foodi Air Fryer and select AIR FRY mode and set the time to 10 minutes at 390 degrees F.
10. Once the cooking cycle completes, take out, and serve.
11. Serve and enjoy.

Serving Suggestion: Serve it with sour cream.

Variation Tip: Use turkey sausages instead of beef sausages.

Nutritional Information Per Serving: Calories 699| Fat 59.1g | Sodium 1217 mg | Carbs 6.8g | Fiber 0.6g| Sugar 2.5g | Protein 33.1 g

Crispy Hash Browns

Prep Time: 10 minutes.
Cook Time: 13 minutes.
Serves: 4

Ingredients:
- 3 russet potatoes
- ¼ cup chopped green peppers
- ¼ cup chopped red peppers
- ¼ cup chopped onions
- 2 garlic cloves chopped
- 1 teaspoon paprika
- Salt and black pepper, to taste
- 2 teaspoons olive oil

Preparation:
1. At 390 degrees F, preheat your Air Fryer on Air Fry mode.
2. Peel and grate all the potatoes with the help of a cheese grater.
3. Add potato shreds to a bowl filled with cold water and leave it soaked for 25 minutes.
4. Drain the water and place the potato shreds on a plate lined with a paper towel.
5. Transfer the shreds to a dry bowl and add olive oil, paprika, garlic, and black pepper.
6. Make four flat patties out of the potato mixture and place them in the Air Fryer Basket.
7. Return the Air Fryer Basket to the Air Fryer and cook for 13 minutes.
8. Initiate cooking by pressing the START/PAUSE BUTTON.
9. Flip the potato hash browns once cooked halfway through, then resume cooking.
10. Once done, serve warm.

Serving Suggestion: Serve the hash with toasted bread slices and crispy bacon.

Variation Tip: Add herbed cream on top of the hash browns.

Nutritional Information Per Serving:
Calories 190 | Fat 18g |Sodium 150mg | Carbs 0.6g | Fiber 0.4g | Sugar 0.4g | Protein 7.2g

Banana and Raisins Muffins

Prep Time: 20 Minutes
Cook Time: 16 Minutes
Serves: 2

Ingredients
- Salt, pinch
- 2 eggs, whisked
- ⅓ cup butter, melted
- 4 tablespoons almond milk
- ¼ teaspoon vanilla extract
- ½ teaspoon baking powder
- 1 ½ cups all-purpose flour
- 1 cup mashed bananas
- 2 tablespoons raisins

Directions
1. Preheat the unit by selecting AIR FRY mode for 3 minutes at 325 degrees F.
2. Select START/PAUSE to begin the preheating process.
3. Once preheating is done, press START/PAUSE.
4. Take about 4 large (one-cup sized) ramekins and layer them with muffin papers.
5. Crack eggs in a large bowl, and whisk it all well and start adding vanilla extract, almond milk, baking powder, and melted butter.
6. Whisk the ingredients very well.
7. Take a separate bowl and add the all-purpose flour, and salt.
8. Now, combine the add dry ingredients with the wet ingredients.
9. Now, pour mashed bananas and raisins into this batter.
10. Mix it well to make a batter for the muffins.
11. Now pour the batter into 4 ramekins and place the ramekins in the air fryer basket.
12. Set the timer to 16 minutes at 350 degrees F at AIR FRY mode.
13. Check if not done, and let it AIR FRY for one more minute.
14. Once it is done, serve.

Serving Suggestion: None
Variation Tip: None
Nutritional Information Per Serving: Calories 727| Fat 43.1g| Sodium 366 mg | Carbs 74.4g | Fiber 4.7g | Sugar 16.1g | Protein 14.1g

Sausage with Eggs

Prep Time: 10 Minutes
Cook Time: 12 Minutes
Serves: 2

Ingredients
- 4 sausage links, raw and uncooked
- 4 eggs, uncooked
- 1 tablespoon green onion
- 2 tablespoons chopped tomatoes
- Salt and black pepper, to taste
- 2 tablespoons milk, dairy
- Oil spray, for greasing

Directions
1. Take a bowl and whisk eggs in it.
2. Then pour milk, and add onions and tomatoes.
3. Whisk it all well.
4. Now season it with salt and black pepper.
5. Take one cake pan, that fit inside the air fryer and grease it with oil spray.
6. Pour the omelet in the greased cake pans.
7. Slice the sausages in round shapes and top it on eggs.
8. Preheat the unit by selecting AIR FRY mode for 3 minutes at 325 degrees F.
9. Select START/PAUSE to begin the preheating process.
10. Once preheating is done, put the cake pan inside the unit.
11. Select Air Fry function of Ninja Air Fryer, and set the timer to 12 minutes at 310 degrees F.
12. Once the cooking cycle completes, serve by transferring it to plates.
13. Enjoy hot as a delicious breakfast.

Serving Suggestion: Serve it with toasted bread slices.
Variation Tip: Use almond milk if like non-dairy milk.
Nutritional Information Per Serving: Calories 240 | Fat 18.4g| Sodium 396mg | Carbs 2.8g | Fiber0.2g | Sugar 2g | Protein 15.6g

Biscuit Balls

Prep Time: 10 minutes.
Cook Time: 18 minutes.
Serves: 6
Ingredients:
- 1 tablespoon butter
- 2 eggs, beaten
- ¼ teaspoon pepper
- 1 can (10.2-oz) Pillsbury Buttermilk biscuits
- 2 ounces cheddar cheese, diced into ten cubes
- Cooking spray
- Egg Wash
- 1 egg
- 1 tablespoon water

Preparation:
1. At 375 degrees F, preheat your Air Fryer on Air Fry mode.
2. Place a suitable non-stick skillet over medium-high heat and cook the bacon until crispy, then place it on a plate lined with a paper towel.
3. Melt butter in the same skillet over medium heat. Beat eggs with pepper in a bowl and pour them into the skillet.
4. Stir cook for 5 minutes, then remove it from the heat.
5. Add bacon and mix well.
6. Divide the dough into 5 biscuits and slice each into 2 layers.
7. Press each biscuit into a 4-inch round.
8. Add a tablespoon of the egg mixture at the center of each round and top it with a piece of cheese.
9. Carefully fold the biscuit dough around the filling and pinch the edges to seal.
10. Whisk egg with water in a small bowl and brush the egg wash over the biscuits.
11. Place the biscuit bombs in the Air Fryer Basket and spray them with cooking oil.
12. Return the Air Fryer Basket to the Air Fryer and cook for 14 minutes.
13. Initiate cooking by pressing the START/PAUSE BUTTON.
14. Flip the egg bombs when cooked halfway through, then resume cooking.
15. Serve warm.

Serving Suggestion: Serve the eggs balls with crispy bacon.
Variation Tip: Add dried herbs to the egg filling.
Nutritional Information Per Serving:
Calories 102 | Fat 7.6g |Sodium 545mg | Carbs 1.5g | Fiber 0.4g | Sugar 0.7g | Protein 7.1g

Breakfast Bacon

Prep Time: 10 minutes.
Cook Time: 14 minutes.
Serves: 4
Ingredients:
- ½ lb. bacon slices

Preparation:
1. At 390 degrees F, preheat your Air Fryer on Air Fry mode.
2. Spread the bacon slices in the Air Fryer Basket evenly in a single layer.
3. Return the Air Fryer Basket to the Air Fryer and cook for 14 minutes.
4. Initiate cooking by pressing the START/PAUSE BUTTON.
5. Flip the crispy bacon once cooked halfway through, then resume cooking.
6. Serve.

Serving Suggestion: Serve the bacon with eggs and bread slices.
Variation Tip: Add salt and black pepper for seasoning.
Nutritional Information Per Serving:
Calories 273 | Fat 22g |Sodium 517mg | Carbs 3.3g | Fiber 0.2g | Sugar 1.4g | Protein 16.1g

Chapter 3-Snacks and Appetizers Recipes

Crispy Tortilla Chips

Prep Time: 15 minutes.
Cook Time: 13 minutes.
Serves: 8

Ingredients:
- 4 (6-inch) corn tortillas
- 1 tablespoon avocado oil
- Sea salt to taste
- Cooking spray

Preparation:
1. At 390 degrees F, preheat your Air Fryer on Air Fry mode.
2. Spread the corn tortillas on the working surface.
3. Slice them into bite-sized triangles.
4. Toss them with salt and cooking oil.
5. Place the triangles in the Air Fryer Basket in a single layer.
6. Return the Air Fryer Basket to the Air Fryer and cook for 13 minutes.
7. Initiate cooking by pressing the START/PAUSE BUTTON.
8. Toss the chips once cooked halfway through, then resume cooking.
9. Serve and enjoy.

Serving Suggestion: Serve with guacamole, mayonnaise, or cream cheese dip.
Variation Tip: Drizzle parmesan cheese on top before air frying.
Nutritional Information Per Serving:
Calories 103 | Fat 8.4g |Sodium 117mg | Carbs 3.5g | Fiber 0.9g | Sugar 1.5g | Protein 5.1g

Chicken Crescent Wraps

Prep Time: 10 minutes.
Cook Time: 12 minutes.
Serves: 6

Ingredients:
- 3 tablespoons chopped onion
- 3 garlic cloves, peeled and minced
- ¾ (8 ounces) package cream cheese
- 6 tablespoons butter
- 2 boneless chicken breasts, cubed, cooked
- 3 (10 ounces) cans of refrigerated crescent roll dough

Preparation:
1. At 390 degrees F, preheat your Air Fryer on Air Fry mode.
2. Heat oil in a skillet and add onion and garlic to sauté until soft.
3. Add cooked chicken, sautéed veggies, butter, and cream cheese to a blender.
4. Blend well until smooth. Spread the crescent dough over a flat surface.
5. Slice the dough into 12 rectangles.
6. Spoon the chicken mixture at the center of each rectangle.
7. Roll the dough to wrap the mixture and form a ball.
8. Place these balls in the Air Fryer Basket.
9. Return the Air Fryer Basket to the Air Fryer and cook for 12 minutes.
10. Initiate cooking by pressing the START/PAUSE BUTTON.
11. Serve warm.

Serving Suggestion: Serve with tomato sauce or cream cheese dip.
Variation Tip: You can also prepare the filling using leftover turkey or pork.
Nutritional Information Per Serving:
Calories 100 | Fat 2g |Sodium 480mg | Carbs 4g | Fiber 2g | Sugar 0g | Protein 18g

Strawberries and Walnuts Muffins

Prep Time: 15 Minutes
Cook Time: 15 Minutes
Serves: 2

Ingredients
- Salt, 1 pinch
- 2 eggs, whisked
- ⅓ cup maple syrup
- ⅓ cup coconut oil
- 4 tablespoons water
- 1 teaspoon orange zest
- ¼ teaspoon vanilla extract
- ½ teaspoon baking powder
- 1 cup all-purpose flour
- 1 cup strawberries, finely chopped
- ⅓ cup walnuts, chopped and roasted

Directions
1. Preheat the unit by selecting AIR FRY mode for 2 minutes at 325 degrees F.
2. Select START/PAUSE to begin the preheating process.
3. Once preheating is done, press START/PAUSE.
4. Take one-cup size of 4 ramekins that are oven safe.
5. Layer it with muffin paper.
6. In a bowl, add egg, maple syrup, oil, water, vanilla extract, and orange zest.
7. Whisk it all very well.
8. In a separate bowl, mix flour, baking powder, and salt.
9. Now add dry ingredients slowly to wet ingredients.
10. Now pour this batter into ramekins and top it with strawberries and walnuts.
11. Now put ramekins inside basket of air fryer and set the time to 15 minutes at 350 degrees F on the AIR FRY mode.
12. Press START/PAUSE to initiate cooking.
13. Check if not done let it AIR FRY for one more minute.
14. Once done, serve.

Serving Suggestion: Serve it with coffee.
Variation Tip: Use vegetable oil instead of coconut oil.
Nutritional Information Per Serving: Calories 897| Fat 53.9g | Sodium 148mg | Carbs 92g | Fiber 4.7g| Sugar35.6 g | Protein 17.5g

Fried Halloumi Cheese

Prep Time: 10 minutes.
Cook Time: 12 minutes.
Serves: 6

Ingredients:
- 1 block halloumi cheese, sliced
- 2 teaspoons olive oil

Preparation:
1. At 360 degrees F, preheat your Air Fryer on Air Fry mode.
2. Place the halloumi cheese slices in the Air Fryer Basket.
3. Drizzle olive oil over the cheese slices.
4. Return the Air Fryer Basket to the Air Fryer and cook for 12 minutes.
5. Flip the cheese slices once cooked halfway through.
6. Serve.

Serving Suggestion: Serve with fresh yogurt dip or cucumber salad.
Variation Tip: Add black pepper and salt for seasoning.
Nutritional Information Per Serving:
Calories 186 | Fat 3g |Sodium 223mg | Carbs 31g | Fiber 8.7g | Sugar 5.5g | Protein 9.7g

Stuffed Bell Peppers

Prep Time: 25 Minutes
Cook Time: 16 Minutes
Serves: 3

Ingredients
- 6 large bell peppers
- 1 ½ cups cooked rice
- 2 cups cheddar cheese

Directions
1. Preheat the unit by selecting AIR FRY mode for 5 minutes at 350 degrees F.
2. Select START/PAUSE to begin the preheating process.
3. Once preheating is done, press START/PAUSE.
4. Cut the bell peppers in half lengthwise and remove all the seeds.
5. Fill the cavity of each bell pepper with cooked rice.
6. Grease the basket of air fryer with oil spray
7. Transfer the bell peppers to the basket of the Ninja Air Fryer.
8. Set the time for 200 degrees F for 10 minutes.
9. Afterward, take out the basket and sprinkle cheese on top.
10. Set the time at 200 degrees F for 6 minutes.
11. Once it's done, serve.

Serving Suggestion: Serve it with mashed potato.
Variation Tip: You can use any cheese you like.
Nutritional Information Per Serving: Calories 605| Fat 26g | Sodium477 mg | Carbs68.3 g | Fiber4 g| Sugar 12.5g | Protein25.6 g

Sweet Bites

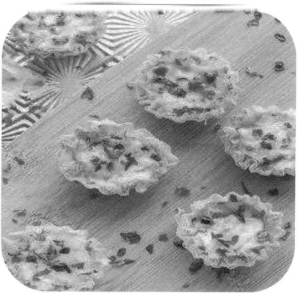

Prep Time: 25 Minutes
Cook Time: 10 Minutes
Serves: 4

Ingredients
- 10 sheets of Phyllo dough, (filo dough)
- 2 tablespoons melted butter
- 1 cup walnuts, chopped
- 2 teaspoons honey
- 1 Pinch cinnamon
- 1 teaspoon orange zest

Directions
1. Preheat the unit by selecting AIR FRY mode for 2 minutes at 325 degrees F.
2. Select START/PAUSE to begin the preheating process.
3. Once preheating is done, press START/PAUSE.
4. First, layer together 10 Phyllo dough sheets on a flat surface.
5. Then cut it into 4*4-inch squares.
6. Now, coat the squares with butter, drizzle some honey, orange zest, walnuts, and cinnamon.
7. Bring all 4 corners together and press the corners to make a little like purse design.
8. Put it inside the air fryer basket and select the AIR FRY mode and set it for 10 minutes at 375 degrees F.
9. Once done, take out and serve.

Serving Suggestion: Serve with a topping of nuts.
Variation Tip: None.
Nutritional Information Per Serving: Calories 397| Fat 27.1 g| Sodium 271mg | Carbs31.2 g | Fiber 3.2g| Sugar3.3g | Protein 11g

Spicy Chicken Tenders

Prep Time: 15 Minutes
Cook Time: 12 Minutes
Serves: 2

Ingredients
- 2 large eggs, whisked
- 2 tablespoons lemon juice
- Salt and black pepper
- 1 pound of chicken tenders
- 1 cup Panko breadcrumbs
- ½ cup Italian bread crumb
- 1 teaspoon smoked paprika
- ¼ teaspoon garlic powder
- ¼ teaspoon onion powder
- ½ cup fresh grated parmesan cheese

Directions
1. Preheat the unit by selecting AIR FRY mode for 2 minutes at 325 degrees F.
2. Select START/PAUSE to begin the preheating process.
3. Once preheating is done, press START/PAUSE.
4. Take a bowl and whisk eggs in it and set aside for further use.
5. In a large bowl add lemon juice, paprika, salt, black pepper, garlic powder, and onion powder.
6. In a separate bowl mix Panko breadcrumbs, Italian bread crumbs, and parmesan cheese.
7. Dip the chicken tenders in the spice mixture and coat the entire tender well.
8. Let the tenders sit for 1 hour.
9. Then dip each chicken tender in egg and then in bread crumbs.
10. Line the basket of the air fryer with parchment paper.
11. Transfer the tenders to the basket.
12. Set it to AIR FRY mode at 350 degrees F for 12 minutes.
13. Once it's done, serve.

Serving Suggestion: Serve it with ketchup.
Variation Tip: Use mild paprika instead of smoked paprika.
Nutritional Information Per Serving: Calories 836| Fat 36g| Sodium1307 mg | Carbs 31.3g | Fiber 2.5g| Sugar3.3 g | Protein 95.3g

Grill Cheese Sandwich

Prep Time: 15 Minutes
Cook Time: 10 Minutes
Serves: 2

Ingredients
- 4 slices white bread slices
- 2 tablespoons of butter, melted
- 2 slices sharp cheddar
- 2 slices Swiss cheese
- 2 slices mozzarella cheese

Directions
1. Preheat the unit by selecting AIR FRY mode for 2 minutes at 325 degrees F.
2. Select START/PAUSE to begin the preheating process.
3. Once preheating is done, press START/PAUSE.
4. Brush melted butter on one side of all the bread slices and then top the 2 bread slices with slices of cheddar, Swiss, and mozzarella, one slice per bread.
5. Top it with the other slice to make a sandwich.
6. Add it to the basket of the air fryer.
7. Turn on AIR FRY mode at 350 degrees F for 10 minutes.
8. Once done, serve.

Serving Suggestion: Serve with tomato soup.
Variation Tip: Use oil spray instead of butter.
Nutritional Information Per Serving: Calories 577 | Fat38g | Sodium 1466mg | Carbs 30.5g | Fiber 1.1g| Sugar 6.5g | Protein 27.6g

Parmesan Crush Chicken

Prep Time: 20 Minutes
Cook Time: 18 Minutes
Serves: 4
Ingredients
- 4 chicken breasts
- 1 cup parmesan cheese
- 1 cup bread crumb
- 2 eggs, whisked
- Salt, to taste
- Oil spray, for greasing

Directions
1. Preheat the unit by selecting AIR FRY mode for 5 minutes at 325 degrees F.
2. Select START/PAUSE to begin the preheating process.
3. Once preheating is done, press START/PAUSE.
4. Whisk egg in a large bowl and set aside.
5. Season the chicken breast with salt and then put it in egg wash.
6. Next, dredge it in breadcrumb then parmesan cheese.
7. Line the basket of the air fryer with parchment paper.
8. Put the breast pieces inside the basket, and oil spray the breast pieces.
9. Set it to AIR FRY mode at 350 degrees F, for 18 minutes.
10. Once it's done, serve.
Serving Suggestion: Serve it with ketchup.
Variation Tip: Use cheddar cheese instead of parmesan.
Nutritional Information Per Serving: Calories 574 | Fat 25g | Sodium 848 mg | Carbs 21.4g | Fiber 1.2g | Sugar 1.8g | Protein 64.4g

Dijon Cheese Sandwich

Prep Time: 10 Minutes
Cook Time: 10 Minutes
Serves: 2
Ingredients
- 4 large slices sourdough, whole grain
- 4 tablespoons of Dijon mustard
- 1 ½ cups grated sharp cheddar cheese
- 2 teaspoons green onion, chopped the green part
- 2 tablespoons butter melted

Directions
1. Preheat the unit by selecting AIR FRY mode for 2 minutes at 325 degrees F.
2. Select START/PAUSE to begin the preheating process.
3. Once preheating is done, press START/PAUSE.
4. Brush the melted butter on one side of all the bread slices.
5. Then spread Dijon mustard on other sides of slices.
6. Then top the 2 bread slices with cheddar cheese and top it with green onions.
7. Cover with the remaining two slices to make two sandwiches.
8. Put it to the basket of the air fryer.
9. Turn on the AIR FRY mode at 350 degrees F, for 10 minutes.
10. Once it's done, serve.
Serving Suggestion: Serve with tomato soup.
Variation Tip: Use oil spray instead of butter.
Nutritional Information Per Serving: calories 617| fat 38 g| sodium 1213mg | carbs 40.8 g | fiber 5g| sugar 5.6g | protein 29.5g

Onion Rings

Prep Time: 10 minutes.
Cook Time: 22 minutes.
Serves: 4
Ingredients:
- ¾ cup all-purpose flour
- 1 teaspoon salt
- 1 large onion, cut into rings
- ½ cup cornstarch
- 2 teaspoons baking powder
- 1 cup low-fat milk
- 1 egg
- 1 cup bread crumbs
- ⅙ teaspoons paprika
- Cooking spray
- ⅙ teaspoons garlic powder

Preparation:
1. At 375 degrees F, preheat your Air Fryer on Air Fry mode.
2. Mix flour with baking powder, cornstarch, and salt in a small bowl.
3. First, coat the onion rings with flour mixture; set them aside.
4. Beat milk with egg, then add the remaining flour mixture into the egg.
5. Mix them well together to make a thick batter.
6. Now dip the floured onion rings into the prepared batter and coat them well.
7. Place the rings on a wire rack for 10 minutes.
8. Spread bread crumbs in a shallow bowl.
9. Coat the onion rings with breadcrumbs and shake off the excess.
10. Set the coated onion rings in the Air Fryer Basket.
11. Spray all the rings with the cooking spray.
12. Return the Air Fryer Basket to the Air Fryer and cook for 22 minutes.
13. Initiate cooking by pressing the START/PAUSE BUTTON.
14. Flip once cooked halfway through, then resume cooking
15. Season the air fried onion rings with garlic powder and paprika.
16. Serve.

Serving Suggestion: Serve with tomato sauce or cream cheese dip.
Variation Tip: Use crushed cornflakes for breading to have extra crispiness.
Nutritional Information Per Serving:
Calories 229 | Fat 1.9 |Sodium 567mg | Carbs 1.9g | Fiber 0.4g | Sugar 0.6g | Protein 11.8g

Peppered Asparagus

Prep Time: 10 minutes.
Cook Time: 16 minutes.
Serves: 6
Ingredients:
- 1 bunch of asparagus, trimmed
- Avocado or olive oil
- Himalayan salt, to taste
- Black pepper, to taste

Preparation:
1. At 390 degrees F, preheat your Air Fryer on Air Fry mode.
2. Place the asparagus in the Air Fryer Basket.
3. Toss the asparagus with salt, black pepper, and oil.
4. Return the Air Fryer Basket to the Air Fryer and cook for 16 minutes.
5. Initiate cooking by pressing the START/PAUSE BUTTON.
6. Serve warm.

Serving Suggestion: Serve with mayonnaise or cream cheese dip.
Variation Tip: Use panko crumbs for breading to have extra crispiness.
Nutritional Information Per Serving:
Calories 163 | Fat 11.5g |Sodium 918mg | Carbs 8.3g | Fiber 4.2g | Sugar 0.2g | Protein 7.4g

Chicken Tenders

Prep Time: 15 Minutes
Cook Time: 12 Minutes
Serves: 3
Ingredients
- 1 pound chicken tender
- Salt and black pepper, to taste
- 1 cup Panko bread crumbs
- 2 cups Italian bread crumbs
- 1 cup parmesan cheese
- 2 eggs
- Oil spray, for greasing

Directions
1. Sprinkle the tenders with salt and black pepper.
2. In a medium bowl, mix Panko bread crumbs with Italian breadcrumbs.
3. Add salt, pepper, and parmesan cheese.
4. Crack two eggs in a bowl.
5. First, put the chicken tender in eggs.
6. Now dredge the tender in a bowl and coat the tender well with crumbs.
7. Preheat the unit by selecting AIR FRY mode for 2 minutes at 325 degrees F.
8. Select START/PAUSE to begin the preheating process.
9. Once preheating is done, press START/PAUSE.
10. Line the basket of the air fryer with parchment paper.
11. At the end, spray the tenders with oil spray.
12. Layer the tenders inside the basket of Ninja Foodi Air Fryer.
13. Set it to the AIR FRY mode at 350 degrees F for 12 minutes.
14. Once it's done, serve.

Serving Suggestion: Serve it with ranch or ketchup.
Variation Tip: Use Italian seasoning instead of Italian bread crumbs.
Nutritional Information Per Serving: Calories558 | Fat23.8g | Sodium872 mg | Carbs 20.9g | Fiber1.7 g| Sugar2.2 g | Protein 63.5g

Crispy Plantain Chips

Prep Time: 15 minutes.
Cook Time: 20 minutes.
Serves: 4
Ingredients:
- 1 green plantain
- 1 teaspoon canola oil
- ½ teaspoons sea salt

Preparation:
1. At 350 degrees F, preheat your Air Fryer on Air Fry mode.
2. Peel and cut the plantains into long strips using a mandolin slicer.
3. Grease the Air Fryer Basket with a ½ teaspoon with canola oil.
4. Toss the plantains with salt and remaining canola oil.
5. Place these plantains in the Air Fryer Basket.
6. Return the Air Fryer Basket to the Air Fryer and cook for 20 minutes.
7. Toss the plantains after 10 minutes and resume cooking.
8. Serve warm.

Serving Suggestion: Serve with cream cheese dip and celery sticks.
Variation Tip: Use black pepper to season the chips.
Nutritional Information Per Serving:
Calories 122 | Fat 1.8g |Sodium 794mg | Carbs 17g | Fiber 8.9g | Sugar 1.6g | Protein 14.9g

Cauliflower Gnocchi

Prep Time: 15 minutes.
Cook Time: 17 minutes.
Serves: 5

Ingredients:
- 1 bag frozen cauliflower gnocchi
- 1 ½ tablespoons olive oil
- 1 teaspoon garlic powder
- 3 tablespoons parmesan, grated
- ½ teaspoon dried basil
- Salt to taste
- Fresh chopped parsley for topping

Preparation:
1. At 400 degrees F, preheat your Air Fryer on Air Fry mode.
2. Toss gnocchi with olive oil, garlic powder, 1 tablespoon of parmesan, salt, and basil in a bowl.
3. Place the gnocchi in the Air Fryer Basket.
4. Return the Air Fryer Basket to the Air Fryer and cook for 10 minutes.
5. Initiate cooking by pressing the START/PAUSE BUTTON.
6. Toss the gnocchi once cooked halfway through, then resume cooking.
7. Drizzle the remaining parmesan on top of the gnocchi and cook again for 7 minutes.
8. Serve warm.

Serving Suggestion: Serve with tomato or sweet chili sauce.
Variation Tip: Use crushed cornflakes for breading to have extra crispiness.
Nutritional Information Per Serving:
Calories 134 | Fat 5.9g |Sodium 343mg | Carbs 9.5g | Fiber 0.5g | Sugar 1.1g | Protein 10.4g

Parmesan French Fries

Prep Time: 10 minutes.
Cook Time: 20 minutes.
Serves: 6

Ingredients:
- 3 medium russet potatoes
- 2 tablespoons parmesan cheese
- 2 tablespoons fresh parsley, chopped
- 1 tablespoon olive oil
- Salt, to taste

Preparation:
1. At 360 degrees F, preheat your Air Fryer on Air Fry mode.
2. Wash the potatoes and pass them through the fries' cutter to get ¼-inch-thick fries.
3. Place the fries in a colander and drizzle salt on top.
4. Leave these fries for 10 minutes, then rinse.
5. Toss the potatoes with parmesan cheese, oil, salt, and parsley in a bowl.
6. Place the potatoes into the Air Fryer Basket.
7. Return the Air Fryer Basket to the Air Fryer and cook for 20 minutes.
8. Initiate cooking by pressing the START/PAUSE BUTTON.
9. Toss the chips once cooked halfway through, then resume cooking.
10. Serve warm.

Serving Suggestion: Serve with tomato ketchup, Asian coleslaw, or creamed cabbage.
Variation Tip: Toss fries with black pepper for change of taste.
Nutritional Information Per Serving:
Calories 307 | Fat 8.6g |Sodium 510mg | Carbs 22.2g | Fiber 1.4g | Sugar 13g | Protein 33.6g

Blueberries Muffins

Prep Time: 15 Minutes
Cook Time: 15 Minutes
Serves: 2

Ingredients
- Salt, pinch
- 2 eggs
- ⅓ cup sugar
- ⅓ cup vegetable oil
- 4 tablespoons water
- 1 teaspoon lemon zest
- ¼ teaspoon vanilla extract
- ½ teaspoon baking powder
- 1 cup all-purpose flour
- 1 cup blueberries

Directions
1. Take 4 one-cup sized ramekins that are oven safe and layer them with muffin papers.
2. Take a bowl and whisk the egg, sugar, oil, water, vanilla extract, and lemon zest.
3. Whisk it all very well.
4. Now, in a separate bowl, mix the flour, baking powder, and salt.
5. Now, add dry ingredients slowly to wet ingredients.
6. Now, pour this batter into ramekins and top it with blueberries.
7. Preheat the unit by selecting AIR FRY mode for 2 minutes at 325 degrees F.
8. Select START/PAUSE to begin the preheating process.
9. Once preheating is done, press START/PAUSE.
10. Now, place the ramekins inside the Ninja Foodi Air Fryer.
11. Set the time to AIR FRY mode for 15 minutes at 350 degrees F.
12. Check if not done, and let it AIR FRY for one more minute.
13. Once it is done, serve.

Serving Suggestion: Serve it with whipped cream topping.
Variation Tip: Use butter instead of vegetable oil.
Nutritional Information Per Serving: Calories 781| Fat41.6g | Sodium 143mg | Carbs 92.7g | Fiber 3.5g| Sugar41.2 g | Protein 0g

Cheddar Quiche

Prep Time: 10 Minutes
Cook Time: 12 Minutes
Serves: 2

Ingredients
- 4 eggs, organic
- 1 ¼ cups heavy cream
- Salt, pinch
- ½ cup broccoli florets
- ½ cup cheddar cheese, shredded and for sprinkling

Directions
1. Take a Pyrex pitcher and crack two eggs in it.
2. And fill it with heavy cream, about half the way up.
3. Add in the salt and then add in the broccoli and pour this into a quiche dish, and top it with shredded cheddar cheese.
4. Preheat the unit by selecting AIR FRY mode for 2 minutes at 325 degrees F.

5. Select START/PAUSE to begin the preheating process.
6. Once preheating is done, press START/PAUSE.
7. Now put the dish inside air fryer basket.
8. Set the time to 12 minutes at 325 degrees F.
9. Once done, serve hot.

Serving Suggestion: Serve with herbs as a topping.

Variation Tip: Use spinach instead of broccoli florets.

Nutritional Information Per Serving: Calories 454| Fat40g | Sodium 406mg | Carbs 4.2g | Fiber 0.6g| Sugar1.3 g | Protein 20g

Potato Tater Tots

Prep Time: 10 minutes.
Cook Time: 27 minutes.
Serves: 4

Ingredients:
- 2 potatoes, peeled
- ½ teaspoon Cajun seasoning
- Olive oil cooking spray
- Sea salt to taste

Preparation:
1. At 375 degrees F, preheat your Air Fryer on Air Fry mode.
2. Boil water in a cooking pot and cook potatoes in it for 15 minutes.
3. Drain and leave the potatoes to cool in a bowl.
4. Grate these potatoes and toss them with Cajun seasoning.
5. Make small tater tots out of this mixture.
6. Place them in the Air Fryer Basket and spray them with cooking oil.
7. Return the Air Fryer Basket to the Air Fryer and cook for 27 minutes.
8. Initiate cooking by pressing the START/PAUSE BUTTON.
9. Flip them once cooked halfway through, and resume cooking.
10. Serve warm.

Serving Suggestion: Serve with ketchup, mayonnaise, or cream cheese dip.

Variation Tip: Use crushed cornflakes for breading to have extra crispiness.

Nutritional Information Per Serving:
Calories 185 | Fat 11g |Sodium 355mg | Carbs 21g | Fiber 5.8g | Sugar 3g | Protein 4.7g

Chicken Stuffed Mushrooms

Prep Time: 15 minutes.
Cook Time: 15 minutes.
Serves: 6

Ingredients:
- 6 large fresh mushrooms, stems removed
- Stuffing:
- ½ cup chicken meat, cubed
- 1 (4 ounces) package cream cheese, softened
- ¼ lb. imitation crabmeat, flaked
- 1 cup butter
- 1 garlic clove, peeled and minced
- Black pepper and salt to taste
- Garlic powder to taste
- Crushed red pepper to taste

Preparation:
1. At 375 degrees F, preheat your Air Fryer on Air Fry mode.
2. Melt and heat butter in a skillet over medium heat.
3. Add chicken and sauté for 5 minutes.
4. Add in all the remaining ingredients for the stuffing.
5. Cook for 5 minutes, then turn off the heat.
6. Allow the mixture to cool. Stuff each mushroom with a tablespoon of this mixture.
7. Place the stuffed mushrooms in the Air Fryer Basket.
8. Return the Air Fryer Basket to the Air Fryer and cook for 15 minutes.
9. Initiate cooking by pressing the START/PAUSE BUTTON.
10. Serve warm.

Serving Suggestion: Serve with mayonnaise or cream cheese dip.
Variation Tip: Use crushed cornflakes for breading to have extra crispiness.
Nutritional Information Per Serving:
Calories 180 | Fat 3.2g | Sodium 133mg | Carbs 32g | Fiber 1.1g | Sugar 1.8g | Protein 9g

Chapter 4-Beef, Lamb and Pork Recipes

Ham Burger Patties

Prep Time: 15 Minutes
Cook Time: 16 Minutes
Serves: 2 Serving
Ingredients
- 1 pound ground beef
- Salt and pepper, to taste
- ½ teaspoon red chili powder
- ¼ teaspoon coriander powder
- 2 tablespoons chopped onion
- 1 green chili, chopped
- Oil spray for greasing
- 2 large potato wedges

Directions
1. Take out the rack and oil greases the air fryer basket with oil spray.
2. Add potato wedges in the basket.
3. Put the rack on top and cover it with aluminum foil.
4. Take a bowl and add minced beef in it and add salt, pepper, chili powder, coriander powder, green chili, and chopped onion.
5. Mix well and make two burger patties with wet hands.
6. Put the patties beside wedges inside air fryer.
7. Now, set time for 12 minutes using AIR FRY mode at 400 degrees F.
8. Once the time of cooking complete, take out the basket.
9. Flip the patties and turn and twist the potatoes wedges.
10. Again, set the air fryer for 4 minutes at 400 degrees F.
11. Once it's done, serve and enjoy.

Serving Suggestion: Serve it with bread slices, cheese, and pickles, lettuce, and onion.
Variation Tip: None.
Nutritional Information Per Serving: Calories875 | Fat21.5g | Sodium 622mg | Carbs 88g | Fiber10.9 g| Sugar 3.4g | Protein 78.8g

Spicy Lamb Chops

Prep Time: 15 Minutes
Cook Time: 15 Minutes
Serves: 4
Ingredients
- 12 lamb chops, bone-in
- Salt and black pepper, to taste
- ½ teaspoon lemon zest
- 1 tablespoon lemon juice
- 1 teaspoon paprika
- 1 teaspoon garlic powder
- ½ teaspoon Italian seasoning
- ¼ teaspoon onion powder

Directions
1. Preheat the unit by selecting AIR FRY mode for 2 minutes at 325 degrees F.
2. Select START/PAUSE to begin the preheating process.
3. Once preheating is done, press START/PAUSE.
4. Add the lamb chops to the bowl and sprinkle salt, garlic powder, Italian seasoning, onion powder, black pepper, lemon zest, lemon juice, and paprika.
5. Rub the chops well, and transfer it to the basket of the air fryer.
6. Set the air fryer at 400 degrees F, for 15 minutes at AIR FRY mode.
7. After 10 minutes, take out the basket and flip the chops.
8. Cook for the remaining minutes, and then serve.

Serving Suggestion: Serve it over rice.
Variation Tip: None.
Nutritional Information Per Serving: Calories 787| Fat 45.3g| Sodium1 mg | Carbs 16.1g | Fiber0.3g | Sugar 0.4g | Protein 75.3g

Short Ribs & Root Vegetables

Prep Time: 15 Minutes
Cook Time: 45 Minutes
Serves: 2

Ingredients
- 1 pound beef short ribs, bone-in and trimmed
- Salt and black pepper, to taste
- 2 tablespoons canola oil, divided
- ¼ cup red wine
- 3 tablespoons brown sugar
- 2 cloves garlic, peeled, minced
- 4 carrots, peeled, cut into 1-inch pieces
- 2 parsnips, peeled, cut into 1-inch pieces
- ½ cup pearl onions

Directions
1. Preheat the unit by selecting AIR FRY mode for 5 minutes at 325 degrees F.
2. Select START/PAUSE to begin the preheating process.
3. Once preheating is done, press START/PAUSE.
4. Season the ribs with salt and black pepper and rub a little amount of canola oil on both sides.
5. Place it in the basket of the air fryer.
6. Next, take a bowl and add pearl onions, parsnip, carrots, garlic, brown sugar, red wine, salt, and black pepper.
7. Add the vegetable mixture over the ribs.
8. Set the time to 45 minutes at 390 degrees F on AIR FRY mode.
9. Hit START/PAUSE so the cooking cycle being.
10. Once the cooking complete, take out the ingredient and serve short ribs with the mixed vegetables and liquid collect at the bottom of basket.
11. Enjoy it hot.

Serving Suggestion: Serve it with mashed potatoes.
Variation Tip: Use olive oil instead of canola oil.
Nutritional Information Per Serving: Calories1262 | Fat 98.6g| Sodium 595mg | Carbs 57g | Fiber 10.1g| Sugar 28.2g | Protein 35.8g

Bell Peppers with Sausages

Prep Time: 15 Minutes
Cook Time: 15 Minutes
Serves: 4

Ingredients
- 6 beef or pork Italian sausages
- 4 bell peppers, whole
- Oil spray, for greasing
- 2 cups cooked rice
- 1 cup sour cream

Directions
1. Preheat the unit by selecting AIR FRY mode for 2 minutes at 325 degrees F.
2. Select START/PAUSE to begin the preheating process.
3. Once preheating is done, press START/PAUSE.
4. Put the bell pepper inside the basket and sausages accommodating aside.
5. Now, place the basket inside the unit.
6. Set it to AIR FRY mode for 15 minutes at 400 degrees F.
7. Once done and serve over cooked rice with a dollop of sour cream.

Serving Suggestion: Serve it with salad.
Variation Tip: Use olive oil instead of oil spray.
Nutritional Information Per Serving: Calories1356 | Fat 81.2g| Sodium 3044 mg | Carbs 96g | Fiber 3.1g | Sugar 8.3g | Protein 57.2 g

Chinese BBQ Pork

Prep Time: 15 Minutes
Cook Time: 25-40 Minutes
Serves: 2

Sauce Ingredients
- 4 tablespoons soy sauce
- ¼ cup red wine
- 2 tablespoons oyster sauce
- ¼ tablespoons hoisin sauce
- ¼ cup honey
- ¼ cup brown sugar
- 1 Pinch salt
- 1 Pinch black pepper
- 1 teaspoon ginger garlic, paste
- 1 teaspoon five-spice powder

Other Ingredients
- 1.5 pounds pork shoulder, sliced

Directions
1. Take a bowl and mix all the ingredients listed under sauce ingredients.
2. Transfer half of it to a sauce pan and let it cook for 10 minutes.
3. Set it aside.
4. Let the pork marinate in the remaining sauce for 2 hours.
5. Afterward, put the pork slices in the basket and set it to AIR FRY mode 400 degrees F for 30 minutes.
6. Make sure the internal temperature is above 160 degrees F once cooked.
7. If not add a few more minutes to the overall cooking time.
8. Once done, take it out and baste it with prepared sauce.
9. Serve and Enjoy.

Serving Suggestion: Serve it with rice.
Variation Tip: Skip the wine and add vinegar.
Nutritional Information Per Serving: Calories 1239| Fat 73 g| Sodium 2185 mg | Carbs 57.3 g | Fiber 0.4g| Sugar53.7 g | Protein 81.5 g

Glazed Steak Recipe

Prep Time: 15 Minutes
Cook Time: 25 Minutes
Serves: 2

Ingredients
- 1 pound of beef steaks
- ½ cup, soy sauce
- Salt and black pepper, to taste
- 1 tablespoon vegetable oil
- 1 teaspoon grated ginger
- 4 cloves garlic, minced
- ¼ cup brown sugar

Directions
1. Take a bowl and whisk together soy sauce, salt, pepper, vegetable oil, garlic, brown sugar, and ginger.
2. Once a paste is made rub the steak with the marinate
3. Let it sit for 30 minutes.
4. After 30 minutes add the steak to the air fryer basket and set it to AIR FRY mode at 400 degrees F for 18-22 minutes.
5. After 10 minutes, hit pause and takeout the basket.
6. Let the steak flip and again let it AIR FRY for the remaining minutes.
7. Once 25 minutes of cooking cycle completes.
8. Take out the steak and let it rest. Serve by cutting into slices.
9. Enjoy.

Serving Suggestion: Serve it with mashed potatoes.
Variation Tip: Use canola oil instead of vegetable oil.
Nutritional Information Per Serving: Calories 563| Fat 21 g| Sodium 156mg | Carbs 20.6g | Fiber0.3 g| Sugar17.8 g | Protein69.4 g

Steak and Mashed Creamy Potatoes

Prep Time: 15 Minutes
Cook Time: 45-50 Minutes
Serves: 1 Serving

Ingredients
- 2 Russet potatoes, peeled and cubed
- ¼ cup butter, divided
- ⅓ cup heavy cream
- ½ cup shredded cheddar cheese
- Salt and black pepper, to taste
- 1 New York strip steak, about a pound
- 1 teaspoon olive oil
- Oil spray, for greasing

Directions
1. Preheat the unit by selecting AIR FRY mode for 5 minutes at 350 degrees F.
2. Select START/PAUSE to begin the preheating process.
3. Once preheating is done, press START/PAUSE.
4. Rub the potatoes with salt and a little amount of olive oil about a teaspoon.
5. Next, season the steak with salt and black pepper.
6. Place the russet potatoes along with steak in basket of air fryer.
7. Oil sprays the steak and set it to AIR FRY mode for 50 minutes, at 375 degrees F.
8. Hit START/PAUSE and let the Ninja Foodi do its magic.
9. One 12 minutes pass, take out the steak and let the cooking cycle completes.
10. Afterward take out potato and mash the potatoes and then add butter, heavy cream, and cheese along with salt and black pepper.
11. Serve the mashed potatoes with steak.
12. Enjoy.

Serving Suggestion: Serve it with rice.
Variation Tip: Use Parmesan instead of cheddar.
Nutritional Information Per Serving: Calories1932 | Fat 85.2g| Sodium 3069mg | Carbs 82g | Fiber10.3 g| Sugar 5.3g | Protein 22.5g

Steak in Air Fry

Prep Time: 15 Minutes
Cook Time: 22 Minutes
Serves: 1 Serving

Ingredients
- 2 teaspoons canola oil
- 1 tablespoon Montreal steaks seasoning
- 1 pound beef steak

Directions
1. Season the steak on both sides with canola oil and then rub a generous amount of steak seasoning all over.
2. Put the steak in the basket and set it to AIR FRY mode at 400 degrees F for 22 minutes.
3. After 7 minutes, hit pause and take out the basket to flip the steak, and cover it with foil on top, for the remaining 14 minutes.
4. Once done, serve the medium-rare steak and enjoy it by resting for 10 minutes.
5. Serve by cutting in slices.
6. Enjoy.

Serving Suggestion: Serve it with mashed potatoes.
Variation Tip: Use vegetable oil instead of canola oil.
Nutritional Information Per Serving: Calories 935| Fat 37.2g| Sodium 1419mg | Carbs 0g | Fiber 0g| Sugar 0g | Protein137.5 g

Beef & Broccoli

Prep Time: 12 Minutes
Cook Time: 12 Minutes
Serves: 4
Ingredients
- 12 ounces teriyaki sauce, divided
- ½ tablespoon garlic powder
- ¼ cup soy sauce
- 1 pound raw sirloin steak, thinly sliced
- 2 cups broccoli, cut into florets
- 2 teaspoons olive oil
- Salt and black pepper, to taste

Directions
1. Preheat the unit by selecting AIR FRY mode for 7 minutes at 350 degrees F.
2. Select START/PAUSE to begin the preheating process.
3. Once preheating is done, press START/PAUSE.
4. Take a zip-lock plastic bag and mix teriyaki sauce, salt, garlic powder, black pepper, soy sauce, and olive oil.
5. Marinate the beef in it for 2 hours.
6. Then drain the beef from the marinade.
7. Now toss the broccoli with oil, teriyaki sauce, and salt and black pepper.
8. Put the ingredients inside the air fryer basket.
9. Set it to AIR FRY mode at 390 degrees F, for 12 minutes.
10. Hit START/PAUSE and let the cooking cycle completes.
11. Once it's done, take out the beef and broccoli and serve immediately with leftover teriyaki sauce and cooked rice.

Serving Suggestion: Serve it with mashed potatoes.
Variation Tip: Use canola oil instead of olive oil.
Nutritional Information Per Serving: Calories 344| Fat 10g| Sodium 4285mg | Carbs18.2 g | Fiber 1.5g| Sugar 13.3g | Protein42 g

Pork Chops

Prep Time: 10 Minutes
Cook Time: 20 Minutes
Serves: 2
Ingredients
- 1 tablespoon rosemary, chopped
- Salt and black pepper, to taste
- 2 garlic cloves
- 1 inch ginger
- 2 tablespoons olive oil
- 8 pork chops

Directions
1. Take a blender and pulse together rosemary, salt, pepper, garlic cloves, ginger, and olive oil.
2. Rub this marinade over pork chops and let it rest for 1 hour.
3. Then adjust it inside the air fryer and set it to AIR FRY mode for 20 minutes at 375 degrees F.
4. Once the cooking cycle is done, take out and serve hot.

Serving Suggestion: Serve it with salad.
Variation Tip: Use canola oil instead of olive oil.
Nutritional Information Per Serving: Calories 1154| Fat 93.8g| Sodium 225mg | Carbs 2.1g| Fiber0.8 g| Sugar 0g | Protein 72.2g

Yogurt Lamb Chops

Prep Time: 10 Minutes
Cook Time: 22 Minutes
Serves: 2
Ingredients
- 1½ cups plain Greek yogurt
- 1 lemon, juice only
- 1 teaspoon ground cumin
- 1 teaspoon ground coriander
- ¾ teaspoon ground turmeric
- ¼ teaspoon ground allspice
- 10 rib lamb chops (1–1¼ inches thick cut)
- 2 tablespoons olive oil, divided

Directions
1. Take a bowl and add lamb chop along with listed ingredients.
2. Rub the lamb chops well and let it marinate in the refrigerator for 1 hour.
3. Afterward takeout the lamb chops from the refrigerator.
4. Layer parchment paper inside basket
5. Put the chops inside basket and place the basket inside the unit.
6. Set the time to 22 minutes at 400 degrees F.
7. Hit start and then wait for the chop to be cooked.
8. Once the cooking is done, take out the lamb chops and let the chops serve on plates.

Serving Suggestion: Serve over rice.
Variation Tip: Use canola oil instead of olive oil.
Nutritional Information Per Serving: Calories1973 | Fat90 g| Sodium228 mg | Carbs 109.2g | Fiber 1g | Sugar 77.5g | Protein 184g

Beef Ribs I

Prep Time: 10 Minutes
Cook Time: 18 Minutes
Serves: 2
Ingredients
- 4 tablespoons barbecue spice rub
- 1 tablespoon kosher salt and black pepper
- 3 tablespoons brown sugar
- 2 pounds beef ribs (3-3 ½ pounds), cut in thirds
- 1 cup barbecue sauce

Directions
1. In a small bowl, add salt, pepper, brown sugar, and BBQ spice rub.
2. Grease the ribs with oil spray from both sides and then rub it with a spice mixture.
3. Adjust the ribs inside the Ninja Air Fryer, and set it to AIR FRY mode at 375 degrees F for 18 minutes.
4. Hit START/PAUSE and let the air fryer cook the ribs.
5. Once done, serve with the coating BBQ sauce.

Serving Suggestion: Serve it with salad and baked potato.
Variation Tip: Use sea salt instead of kosher salt.
Nutritional Information Per Serving: Calories1081 | Fat 28.6 g| Sodium 1701mg | Carbs 58g | Fiber 0.8g| Sugar 45.7g | Protein 138 g

Beef Ribs II

Prep Time: 20 Minutes
Cook Time: 1 Hour
Serves: 2

Ingredients for Marinade
- ¼ cup olive oil
- 4 garlic cloves, minced
- ½ cup white wine vinegar
- ¼ cup soy sauce, reduced-sodium
- ¼ cup Worcestershire sauce
- 1 lemon juice
- Salt and black pepper, to taste
- 2 tablespoons Italian seasoning
- 1 teaspoon smoked paprika
- 2 tablespoons mustard
- ½ cup maple syrup

Meat Ingredients
- Oil spray, for greasing
- 8 beef ribs lean

Directions
1. Preheat the unit by selecting AIR FRY mode for 2 minutes at 325 degrees F.
2. Select START/PAUSE to begin the preheating process.
3. Once preheating is done, press START/PAUSE.
1. Take a large bowl and add all the ingredients under marinade ingredients.
2. Put the marinade in a zip lock bag and add ribs to it.
3. Let it sit for 4 hours.
4. Now take out the basket of air fryer and grease the basket with oil spray.
5. Now put the ribs in the basket.
6. Set it to AIR FRY mode at 220 degrees F for 30 minutes.
7. Select Pause and take out the basket.
8. Afterward, flip the ribs and cook for 30 more minutes at 250 degrees F.
9. Once done, serve the juicy and tender ribs.
10. Enjoy.

Serving Suggestion: Serve it with Mac and cheese.
Variation Tip: Use garlic-infused oil instead of garlic cloves.
Nutritional Information Per Serving: Calories 1927| Fat116g| Sodium 1394mg | Carbs 35.2g | Fiber 1.3g| Sugar29 g | Protein 172.3g

Chipotle Beef

Prep Time: 15 minutes.
Cook Time: 18 minutes.
Serves: 4

Ingredients:
- 1 lb. beef steak, cut into chunks
- 1 large egg
- ½ cup parmesan cheese, grated
- ½ cup pork panko
- ½ teaspoon seasoned salt

Chipotle Ranch Dip
- ¼ cup mayonnaise
- ¼ cup sour cream
- 1 teaspoon chipotle paste
- ½ teaspoon ranch dressing mix
- ¼ medium lime, juiced

Preparation:
1. At 390 degrees F, preheat your Air Fryer on Air Fry mode.
2. Mix all the ingredients for chipotle ranch dip in a bowl.
3. Keep it in the refrigerator for 30 minutes.
4. Mix pork panko with salt and parmesan.
5. Beat egg in one bowl and spread the panko mixture in another flat bowl.
6. Dip the steak chunks in the egg first, then coat them with panko mixture.

7. Spread them in the Air Fryer Basket and spray them with cooking oil.
8. Return the Air Fryer Basket to the Air Fryer and cook for 18 minutes.
9. Initiate cooking by pressing the START/PAUSE BUTTON.
10. Serve with chipotle ranch and salt and pepper on top. Enjoy.

Serving Suggestion: Serve with tomato ketchup or chili sauce.
Variation Tip: Add crushed cornflakes for breading to get extra crisp.
Nutritional Information Per Serving:
Calories 310 | Fat 17g |Sodium 271mg | Carbs 4.3g | Fiber 0.9g | Sugar 2.1g | Protein 35g

Zucchini Pork Skewers

Prep Time: 15 minutes.
Cook Time: 23 minutes.
Serves: 4
Ingredients:
- 1 large zucchini, cut 1" pieces
- 1 lb. boneless pork belly, cut into cubes
- 1 onion yellow, diced in squares
- 1 ½ cups grape tomatoes
- 1 garlic clove minced
- 1 lemon, juice only
- ¼ cup olive oil
- 2 tablespoons balsamic vinegar
- 1 teaspoon oregano
- olive oil spray

Preparation:
1. At 390 degrees F, preheat your Air Fryer on Air Fry mode.
2. Mix together balsamic vinegar, garlic, oregano lemon juice, and ¼ cup of olive oil in a suitable bowl.
3. Then toss in diced pork pieces and mix well to coat.
4. Leave the seasoned pork to marinate for 60 minutes in the refrigerator.
5. Take suitable wooden skewers for your Air Fryer's Basket, and then thread marinated pork and vegetables on each skewer in an alternating manner.
6. Place the skewers in the Air Fryer Basket and spray them with cooking oil.
7. Return the Air Fryer Basket to the Air Fryer and cook for 23 minutes.
8. Initiate cooking by pressing the START/PAUSE BUTTON.
9. Flip the skewers once cooked halfway through, and resume cooking.
10. Serve warm.

Serving Suggestion: Serve with sautéed green beans and cherry tomatoes.
Variation Tip: Use honey glaze to baste the skewers.
Nutritional Information Per Serving:
Calories 459 | Fat 17.7g |Sodium 1516mg | Carbs 1.7g | Fiber 0.5g | Sugar 0.4g | Protein 69.2g

Mustard Rubbed Lamb Chops

Prep Time: 15 minutes.
Cook Time: 32 minutes.
Serves: 4
Ingredients:
- 1 teaspoon Dijon mustard
- 1 teaspoon olive oil
- ½ teaspoon soy sauce
- ½ teaspoon garlic, minced
- ½ teaspoon cumin powder
- ½ teaspoon cayenne pepper

- ½ teaspoon Italian spice blend
- ⅛ teaspoon salt
- 4 pieces of lamb chops

Preparation:
1. At 350 degrees F, preheat your Air Fryer on Air Fry mode.
2. Mix Dijon mustard, soy sauce, olive oil, garlic, cumin powder, cayenne pepper, Italian spice blend, and salt in a medium bowl and mix well.
3. Place lamb chops into a Ziploc bag and pour in the marinade.
4. Press the air out of the bag and seal tightly.
5. Press the marinade around the lamb chops to coat.
6. Keep then in the fridge and marinate for at least 30 minutes, up to overnight.
7. Place the chops in the Air Fryer Basket and spray them with cooking oil.
8. Return the Air Fryer Basket to the Air Fryer and cook for 27 minutes.
9. Initiate cooking by pressing the START/PAUSE BUTTON.
10. Flip the chops once cooked halfway through, and resume cooking.
11. Switch the Air fryer to AIR broil mode and cook for 5 minutes.
12. Serve warm.

Serving Suggestion: Serve the chops with a dollop of cream cheese dip on top.
Variation Tip: Rub the lamb chops with balsamic vinegar or honey before seasoning.
Nutritional Information Per Serving:
Calories 264 | Fat 17g |Sodium 129mg | Carbs 0.9g | Fiber 0.3g | Sugar 0g | Protein 27g

Air Fryer Meatloaves

Prep Time: 10 minutes.
Cook Time: 22 minutes.
Serves: 4
Ingredients:
- ⅓ cup milk
- 2 tablespoons basil pesto
- 1 egg, beaten
- 1 garlic clove, minced
- ¼ teaspoon black pepper
- 1 lb. ground beef
- ⅓ cup panko bread crumbs
- 8 pepperoni slices
- ½ cup marinara sauce, warmed
- 1 tablespoon fresh basil, chopped

Preparation:
1. At 390 degrees F, preheat your Air Fryer on Air Fry mode.
2. Mix pesto, milk, egg, garlic, and black pepper in a medium-sized bowl.
3. Stir in ground beef and bread crumbs, then mix.
4. Make the 4 small-sized loaves with this mixture and top them with 2 pepperoni slices.
5. Press the slices into the meatloaves.
6. Place the meatloaves in the Air Fryer Basket.
7. Return the Air Fryer Basket to the Air Fryer and cook for 22 minutes.
8. Initiate cooking by pressing the START/PAUSE BUTTON.
9. Top them with marinara sauce and basil to serve.
10. Serve warm.

Serving Suggestion: Serve with avocado dip.
Variation Tip: Add finely chopped carrots and zucchini to the meatloaf.
Nutritional Information Per Serving:
Calories 316 | Fat 12.2g |Sodium 587mg | Carbs 12.2g | Fiber 1g | Sugar 1.8g | Protein 25.8g

Lamb Shank with Mushroom Sauce

Prep Time: 15 minutes.
Cook Time: 35 minutes.
Serves: 4
Ingredients:
- 20 mushrooms, chopped
- 2 red bell pepper, chopped
- 2 red onion, chopped
- 1 cup red wine
- 4 leeks, chopped

- 6 tablespoons balsamic vinegar
- 2 teaspoons black pepper
- 2 teaspoons salt
- 3 tablespoons fresh rosemary
- 6 garlic cloves
- 4 lamb shanks
- 3 tablespoons olive oil

Preparation:
1. At 390 degrees F, preheat your Air Fryer on Air Fry mode.
2. Season the lamb shanks with salt, pepper, rosemary, and 1 teaspoon of olive oil.
3. Set the shanks in the Air Fryer Basket.
4. Return the Air Fryer Basket to the Air Fryer and cook for 25 minutes.
5. Initiate cooking by pressing the START/PAUSE BUTTON.
6. Flip the shanks halfway through, and resume cooking.
7. Meanwhile, add and heat the remaining olive oil in a skillet.
8. Add onion and garlic to sauté for 5 minutes.
9. Add in mushrooms and cook for 5 minutes.
10. Add red wine and cook until it is absorbed
11. Stir all the remaining vegetables along with black pepper and salt.
12. Cook until vegetables are al dente.
13. Serve the air fried shanks with sautéed vegetable fry.

Serving Suggestion: Serve with sautéed zucchini and green beans.
Variation Tip: Rub the lamb shanks with lemon juice before seasoning.
Nutritional Information Per Serving:
Calories 352 | Fat 9.1g |Sodium 1294mg | Carbs 3.9g | Fiber 1g | Sugar 1g | Protein 61g

Parmesan Pork Chops

Prep Time: 10 minutes.
Cook Time: 15 minutes.
Serves: 4
Ingredients:
- 4 boneless pork chops
- 2 tablespoons olive oil
- ½ cup freshly grated Parmesan
- 1 teaspoon salt
- 1 teaspoon paprika
- 1 teaspoon garlic powder
- 1 teaspoon onion powder
- ½ teaspoon black pepper

Preparation:
1. At 390 degrees F, preheat your Air Fryer on Air Fry mode.
2. Pat dry the pork chops with a paper towel and rub them with olive oil.
3. Mix parmesan with spices in a medium bowl.
4. Rub the pork chops with Parmesan mixture.
5. Place the seasoned pork chops in the Air Fryer Basket.
6. Return the Air Fryer Basket to the Air Fryer and cook for 15 minutes.
7. Initiate cooking by pressing the START/PAUSE BUTTON.
8. Flip the pork chops when cooked halfway through, then resume cooking.
9. Serve warm.

Serving Suggestion: Serve boiled rice or steamed cauliflower rice.
Variation Tip: Rub the chops with garlic cloves before seasoning.
Nutritional Information Per Serving:
Calories 396 | Fat 23.2g |Sodium 622mg | Carbs 0.7g | Fiber 0g | Sugar 0g | Protein 45.6g

Pork Chops with Broccoli

Prep Time: 15 minutes.
Cook Time: 21 minutes.
Serves: 2
Ingredients:
- 2 (5 ounces) bone-in pork chops
- 2 tablespoons avocado oil

- ½ teaspoon paprika
- ½ teaspoon onion powder
- ½ teaspoon garlic powder
- 1 teaspoon salt
- 2 cups broccoli florets
- 2 garlic cloves, minced

Preparation:
1. At 375 degrees F, preheat your Air Fryer on Air Fry mode.
2. Rub the pork chops with avocado oil, garlic, paprika, and spices.
3. Add pork chops to the Air Fryer Basket.
4. Return the Air Fryer Basket to the Air Fryer and cook for 15 minutes.
5. Transfer the chops to a plate and keep them covered.
6. Add the broccoli to the Air Fryer Basket and return it to the unit.
7. Choose the Air Fryer mode with 375 degrees F temperature and 6 minutes cooking time.
8. Initiate cooking by pressing the START/PAUSE BUTTON.
9. Flip the pork once cooked halfway through.
10. Cut the hardened butter into the cubes and place them on top of the pork chops.
11. Serve warm with crispy broccoli florets.

Serving Suggestion: Serve with warm corn tortilla and crouton salad.

Variation Tip: Rub the pork chops with garlic cloves before seasoning.

Nutritional Information Per Serving:
Calories 410 | Fat 17.8g | Sodium 619mg | Carbs 21g | Fiber 1.4g | Sugar 1.8g | Protein 38.4g

Turkey and Beef Meatballs

Prep Time: 15 minutes.
Cook Time: 24 minutes.
Serves: 6

Ingredients:
- 1 medium shallot, minced
- 2 tablespoons olive oil
- 3 garlic cloves, minced
- ¼ cup panko crumbs
- 2 tablespoons whole milk
- ⅔ lb. lean ground beef
- ⅓ lb. bulk turkey sausage
- 1 large egg, lightly beaten
- ¼ cup parsley, chopped
- 1 tablespoon fresh thyme, chopped
- 1 tablespoon fresh rosemary, chopped
- 1 tablespoon Dijon mustard
- ½ teaspoon salt

Preparation:
1. At 400 degrees F, preheat your Air Fryer on Air Fry mode.
2. Place a medium non-stick pan over medium-high heat.
3. Add oil and shallot, then sauté for 2 minutes.
4. Toss in the garlic and cook for 1 minute.
5. Remove this pan from the heat.
6. Whisk panko with milk in a large bowl and leave it for 5 minutes.
7. Add cooked shallot mixture and mix well.
8. Stir in egg, parsley, turkey sausage, beef, thyme, rosemary, salt, and mustard.
9. Mix well, then divide the mixture into 1 ½ inches balls.
10. Place these balls in the Air Fryer Basket and spray them with cooking oil.
11. Return the Air Fryer Basket to the Air Fryer and cook for 21 minutes.
12. Initiate cooking by pressing the START/PAUSE BUTTON.
13. Serve warm.

Serving Suggestion: Serve with fresh vegetable salad and marinara sauce.

Variation Tip: Add freshly chopped parsley and coriander for change of taste.

Nutritional Information Per Serving:
Calories 551 | Fat 31g | Sodium 1329mg | Carbs 1.5g | Fiber 0.8g | Sugar 0.4g | Protein 64g

Pork with Green Beans and Potatoes

Prep Time: 10 minutes.
Cook Time: 25 minutes.
Serves: 4

Ingredients:
- ¼ cup Dijon mustard
- 2 tablespoons brown sugar
- 1 teaspoon dried parsley flake
- ½ teaspoon dried thyme
- ¼ teaspoon salt
- ¼ teaspoon black pepper
- 1 ¼ lbs. pork tenderloin
- ¾ lb. small potatoes halved
- 1 (12-oz) package green beans, trimmed
- 1 tablespoon olive oil
- Salt and black pepper ground to taste

Preparation:
1. At 350 degrees F, preheat your Air Fryer on Air Fry mode.
2. Add mustard, parsley, brown sugar, salt, black pepper, and thyme in a large bowl, then mix well.
3. Add tenderloin to the spice mixture and coat well.
4. Toss potatoes with olive oil, salt, black pepper, and green beans in another bowl.
5. Place the prepared tenderloin in the Air Fryer Basket.
6. Return the Air Fryer Basket to the Air Fryer and cook for 15 minutes.
7. Transfer the tenderloin to a plate and keep it covered.
8. Add potatoes and green beans to the Air Fryer Basket.
9. Choose the Air Fryer mode with 350 degrees F temperature and 10 minutes cooking time.
10. Initiate cooking by pressing the START/PAUSE BUTTON.
11. Serve the tenderloin with Air Fried potatoes.

Serving Suggestion: Serve with sautéed leeks or cabbages.
Variation Tip: Rub the tenderloins with garlic cloves before seasoning.
Nutritional Information Per Serving:
Calories 400 | Fat 32g | Sodium 721mg | Carbs 2.6g | Fiber 0g | Sugar 0g | Protein 27.4g

Gochujang Brisket

Prep Time: 20 minutes.
Cook Time: 55 minutes.
Serves: 6

Ingredients:
- ½ tablespoon sweet paprika
- ½ teaspoon toasted sesame oil
- 2 lbs. beef brisket, cut into 4 pieces
- Salt, to taste
- ⅛ cup Gochujang, Korean chili paste
- Black pepper, to taste
- 1 small onion, diced
- 2 garlic cloves, minced
- 1 teaspoon Asian fish sauce
- 1 ½ tablespoons peanut oil, as needed
- ½ tablespoons fresh ginger, grated
- ¼ teaspoon red chili flakes
- ½ cup water
- 1 tablespoon ketchup
- 1 tablespoon soy sauce

Preparation:
1. At 390 degrees F, preheat your Air Fryer on Air Fry mode.
2. Thoroughly rub the beef brisket with olive oil, paprika, chili flakes, black pepper, and salt.
3. Place the brisket in the Air Fryer Basket.
4. Return the Air Fryer Basket to the Air Fryer and cook for 35 minutes.
5. Initiate cooking by pressing the START/PAUSE BUTTON.

6. Flip the brisket halfway through, and resume cooking.
7. Meanwhile, heat oil in a skillet and add ginger, onion, and garlic.
8. Sauté for 5 minutes, then add all the remaining ingredients.
9. Cook the mixture for 15 minutes approximately until well thoroughly mixed.
10. Serve the brisket with this sauce on top.

Serving Suggestion: Serve on top of boiled white rice.
Variation Tip: Add Worcestershire sauce and honey to taste.
Nutritional Information Per Serving:
Calories 374 | Fat 25g | Sodium 275mg | Carbs 7.3g | Fiber 0g | Sugar 6g | Protein 12.3g

Beef Cheeseburgers

Prep Time: 15 minutes.
Cook Time: 13 minutes.
Serves: 4
Ingredients:
- 1 lb. ground beef
- Salt, to taste
- 2 garlic cloves, minced
- 1 tablespoon soy sauce
- Black pepper, to taste
- 4 American cheese slices
- 4 hamburger buns
- Mayonnaise, to serve
- Lettuce, to serve
- Sliced tomatoes, to serve
- Sliced red onion, to serve

Preparation:
1. At 390 degrees F, preheat your Air Fryer on Air Fry mode.
2. Mix beef with soy sauce and garlic in a large bowl.
3. Make 4 patties of 4 inches in diameter.
4. Rub them with salt and black pepper on both sides.
5. Place the patties in the Air Fryer Basket.
6. Return the Air Fryer Basket to the Air Fryer and cook for 13 minutes.
7. Initiate cooking by pressing the START/PAUSE BUTTON.
8. Flip each patty once cooked halfway through, and resume cooking.
9. Add each patty to the hamburger buns along with mayo, tomatoes, onions, and lettuce.
10. Serve.

Serving Suggestion: Serve with tomato ketchup or chili sauce.
Variation Tip: Add breadcrumbs to the beef burger mixture for a crumbly texture.
Nutritional Information Per Serving:
Calories 437 | Fat 28g | Sodium 1221mg | Carbs 22.3g | Fiber 0.9g | Sugar 8g | Protein 30.3g

Pork Chops with Brussels Sprouts

Prep Time: 15 minutes.
Cook Time: 28 minutes.
Serves: 4

Ingredients:
- 4 bone-in center-cut pork chop
- Cooking spray
- Salt, to taste
- Black pepper, to taste
- 2 teaspoons olive oil
- 2 teaspoons pure maple syrup
- 2 teaspoons Dijon mustard
- 6 ounces Brussels sprouts, quartered

Preparation:
1. At 350 degrees F, preheat your Air Fryer on Air Fry mode.
2. Rub pork chop with salt, ¼ teaspoon of black pepper, and cooking spray.
3. Toss brussels sprouts with mustard, syrup, oil, ¼ teaspoon of black pepper in a medium bowl.
4. Add pork chops to the Air Fryer Basket.
5. Return the Air Fryer Basket to the Air Fryer and cook for 15 minutes.
6. Transfer the pork chops to a plate and keep them covered.
7. Add the brussels sprouts to the basket and return it to the unit.
8. Choose the Air Fryer mode with 350 degrees F temperature and 13 minutes cooking time.
9. Initiate cooking by pressing the START/PAUSE BUTTON.
10. Serve warm and fresh.

Serving Suggestion: Serve with Greek salad and crispy bread.
Variation Tip: Rub the pork chops with garlic cloves before seasoning.
Nutritional Information Per Serving:
Calories 336 | Fat 27.1g |Sodium 66mg | Carbs 1.1g | Fiber 0.4g | Sugar 0.2g | Protein 19.7g

Chapter 5-Chicken and Poultry Recipes

Glazed Thighs with French Fries

Prep Time: 22 Minutes
Cook Time: 35 Minutes
Serves: 3

Ingredients
- 2 tablespoons soy sauce
- Salt, to taste
- 1 teaspoon Worcestershire Sauce
- 2 teaspoons Brown Sugar
- 1 teaspoon ginger, paste
- 1 teaspoon garlic, paste
- 6 boneless chicken thighs
- 1 pound of hand-cut potato fries (thick)
- 2 tablespoons canola oil

Directions
1. Coat the French fries well with canola oil.
2. Season it with salt.
3. In a small bowl, combine the soy sauce, Worcestershire sauce, brown sugar, ginger, and garlic.
4. Place the chicken in this marinade and let it sit for 40 minutes.
5. Put the chicken thighs and potatoes into the basket.
6. Set it to AIR FRY mode at 390 degrees F for 25-35 minutes.
7. Once the cooking cycle completely take out the fries and chicken and serve it hot.

Serving Suggestion: Serve it with ketchup.
Variation Tip: You can use honey instead of brown sugar.
Nutritional Information Per Serving: Calories 858| Fat39g | Sodium 1509mg | Carbs 45.6g | Fiber 4.4g | Sugar3 g | Protein 90g

Balsamic Duck Breast

Prep Time: 15 minutes.
Cook Time: 20 minutes.
Serves: 2

Ingredients:
- 2 Duck Breasts
- 1 teaspoon parsley
- Salt and black pepper, to taste

Marinade:
- 1 tablespoon olive oil
- ½ teaspoon French mustard
- 1 teaspoon dried garlic
- 2 teaspoons honey
- ½ teaspoon balsamic vinegar

Preparation:
1. At 360 degrees F, preheat your Air Fryer on Air Fry mode.
2. Mix olive oil, mustard, garlic, honey, and balsamic vinegar in a bowl.
3. Add duck breasts to the marinade and rub well.
4. Place one duck breast in the Air Fryer Basket.
5. Return the Air Fryer Basket to the Air Fryer and cook for 20 minutes.
6. Initiate cooking by pressing the START/PAUSE BUTTON.
7. Flip the duck breasts once cooked halfway through, then resume cooking.
8. Serve warm.

Serving Suggestion: Serve with white rice and avocado salad
Variation Tip: Rub the duck breast with garlic cloves before seasoning.
Nutritional Information Per Serving:
Calories 546 | Fat 33.1g |Sodium 1201mg | Carbs 30g | Fiber 2.4g | Sugar 9.7g | Protein 32g

Sweet and Spicy Carrots with Chicken Thighs

Prep Time: 15 Minutes
Cook Time: 25 Minutes
Serves: 2
Ingredients
Ingredients for Glaze
- Cooking spray, for greasing
- 2 tablespoons butter, melted
- 1 tablespoon hot honey
- 1 teaspoon orange zest
- 1 teaspoon cardamom
- ½ pound baby carrots
- 1 tablespoon orange juice
- Salt and black pepper, to taste

Other Ingredients
- ½ pound carrots, baby carrots
- 8 chicken thighs

Directions
1. Take a bowl and mix all the glaze ingredients in it.
2. Now, coat the chicken and carrots with the glaze and let it rest for 30 minutes.
3. Now place the chicken thighs and carrots into the air fryer basket.
4. Press start and set it to ROAST mode at 390 degrees F for 25 minutes.
5. After 12 minutes, take out the carrots and let the cooking cycle completes for chicken.
6. Then serve it hot.
Serving Suggestion: Serve with Salad.
Variation Tip: Use lime juice instead of orange juice.
Nutritional Information Per Serving: Calories 1312| Fat 55.4g| Sodium 757mg | Carbs 23.3g | Fiber6.7 g | Sugar12 g | Protein171 g

Wings with Corn on Cob

Prep Time: 15 Minutes
Cook Time: 25 Minutes
Serves: 2
Ingredients
- 6 chicken wings, skinless
- 2 tablespoons coconut amino
- 2 tablespoons brown sugar
- 1 teaspoon ginger, paste
- ½ inch garlic, minced
- Salt and black pepper to taste
- 2 corn on cobs, small
- Oil spray, for greasing

Directions
1. Spay the corns with oil spray and season them with salt.
2. Rub the ingredients well.
3. Coat the chicken wings with coconut amino, brown sugar, ginger, garlic, salt, and black pepper.
4. Spray the wings with a good amount of oil spray.

5. Now put the chicken wings in the basket, along with corns.
6. Select AIR FRY function and set time to 25 minutes at 390 degrees F.
7. After 15 minutes take out the corn.
8. Let the cooking cycle complete for the chicken.
9. Once it's done, serve and enjoy.
Serving Suggestion: Serve it with garlic butter sauce.
Variation Tip: Use butter instead of oil spray.
Nutritional Information Per Serving: Calories 950| Fat33.4g | Sodium592 mg | Carbs27.4g | Fiber2.1g | Sugar11.3 g | Protein129 g

Yummy Chicken Breasts

Prep Time: 15 Minutes
Cook Time: 25 Minutes
Serves: 2
Ingredients
- 4 large chicken breasts, 6 ounces each
- 2 tablespoons oil bay seasoning
- 1 tablespoon Montreal chicken seasoning
- 1 teaspoon thyme
- ½ teaspoon paprika
- Salt, to taste
- oil spray, for greasing

Directions
1. Season the chicken breast pieces with the listed seasoning and let them rest for 40 minutes.
2. Grease both sides of the chicken breast pieces with oil spray.
3. Put the chicken breast pieces inside the basket.
4. Set the AIR FRY mode at 400 degrees F, for 15 minutes.
5. Select pause and take out the basket and flip the chicken breast pieces, after 15 minutes.
6. Select AIR FRY at 400 degrees F, for 10 more minutes.
7. Once it's done serve.
Serving Suggestion: Serve it with baked potato.
Variation Tip: None
Nutritional Information Per Serving: Calories 711| Fat 27.7g| Sodium 895mg | Carbs 1.6g | Fiber 0.4g | Sugar 0.1g | Protein 106.3g

Chicken Thighs with Brussels sprouts

Prep Time: 20 Minutes
Cook Time: 30 Minutes
Serves: 2
Ingredients
- 2 tablespoons honey
- 4 tablespoons Dijon mustard
- Salt and black pepper, to tat
- 4 tablespoons olive oil
- 1-½ cup Brussels sprouts
- 8 chicken thighs, skinless

Directions
1. Take a bowl and add chicken thighs to it.
2. Add honey, Dijon mustard, salt, pepper, and 2 tablespoons of olive oil to the thighs.
3. Coat the chicken well and marinate it for 1 hour.
4. Now when start cooking season the Brussels sprouts with salt and black pepper along with remaining olive oil.
5. Put the chicken along with the Brussels sprouts into the basket.
6. Select ROAST function and set time to 30 minutes at 390 degrees F.
7. Once done, serve and enjoy.

Serving Suggestion: Serve it with Barbecue Sauce.
Variation Tip: You can use canola oil instead of olive oil.
Nutritional Information Per Serving: Calories 1454 | Fat 72.2g | Sodium 869mg | Carbs 23g | Fiber 2.7g | Sugar 19g | Protein 172g

Chicken & Broccoli

Prep Time: 22 Minutes
Cook Time: 22 Minutes
Serves: 2

Ingredients
- 1 pound chicken, boneless & bite-size pieces
- 1 ½ cups broccoli
- 2 tablespoons Grape seed oil
- ⅓ teaspoon garlic powder
- 1 teaspoon ginger and garlic paste
- 2 teaspoons soy sauce
- 1 tablespoon sesame seed oil
- 2 teaspoons rice vinegar
- Salt and black pepper, to taste
- Oil spray, for coating

Directions
1. Take a small bowl and whisk together grape seed oil, ginger and garlic paste, sesame seeds oil, rice vinegar, and soy sauce.
2. Take a large bowl and mix chicken pieces with the prepared marinade.
3. Let it sit for 1 hour.
4. Now, slightly grease the broccoli with oil spray and season it with salt and black pepper.
5. Put the broccoli and chicken into the basket of the air fryer that is greased with oil spray.
6. Set it to AIR FRY mode at 390 degrees F, for 22 minutes.
7. After 8 minutes of cooking, press the START/PAUSE button and takes out the broccoli.
8. Keep continuing with the chicken cooking process.
9. Once the cooking time completes, take out the chicken and serve it with the broccoli.
Serving Suggestion: Serve it with lemon wedges.
Variation Tip: A light oil alternative can be used as grape seed oil.
Nutritional Information Per Serving: Calories 588 | Fat 32.1g | Sodium 457mg | Carbs 4g | Fiber 1.3 g | Sugar 1g | Protein 67.4 g

Chicken Leg Piece

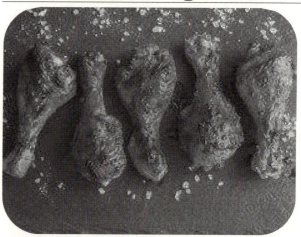

Prep Time: 15 Minutes
Cook Time: 25 Minutes
Serves: 1 Serving

Ingredients
- 1 teaspoon onion powder
- 1 teaspoon paprika powder
- 1 teaspoon garlic powder
- Salt and black pepper, to taste
- 1 tablespoon Italian seasoning
- 1 teaspoon celery seeds
- 2 eggs, whisked
- ⅓ cup buttermilk
- 1 cup corn flour
- 1 pound chicken leg

Directions
1. Take a bowl and whisk egg along with pepper, salt, and buttermilk.
2. Set it aside for further use.
3. Mix all the spices in a small separate bowl.
4. Dredge the chicken in egg wash then dredge it in seasoning.
5. Coat the chicken legs with oil spray.
6. At the end dust it with the corn flour.
7. Put the leg pieces into air fryer basket.
8. Set it to 400 degrees F, for 25 minutes.
9. Let the air fryer do the magic.
10. Once it's done, serve and enjoy.
Serving Suggestion: Serve it with cooked rice.
Variation Tip: Use water instead of buttermilk.

Nutritional Information Per Serving: Calories 1511| Fat 52.3g| Sodium 615 mg | Carbs 100g | Fiber 9.2g | Sugar 8.1g | Protein 154.2g

Spiced Chicken and Vegetables

Prep Time: 22 Minutes
Cook Time: 35 Minutes
Serves: 1 Serving
Ingredients
- 2 large chicken breasts
- 2 teaspoons olive oil
- 1 teaspoon chili powder
- 1 teaspoon paprika powder
- 1 teaspoon onion powder
- ½ teaspoon garlic powder
- ¼ teaspoon Cumin
- Salt and black pepper, to taste

Vegetable Ingredients
- 2 large potato, cubed
- 4 large carrots cut into bite-size pieces
- 1 tablespoon olive oil
- Salt and black pepper, to taste

Directions
1. Take chicken breast pieces and rub olive oil, salt, pepper, chili powder, onion powder, cumin, garlic powder, and paprika.
2. Season the vegetables with olive oil, salt, and black pepper.
3. Now put the chicken breast pieces along with vegetables inside the air fryer basket.
4. Now set it to AIR FRY mode at 390 degrees F, for 35 minutes.
5. Once the cooking cycle is done, serve, and enjoy.

Serving Suggestion: Serve it with salad or ranch dressing.

Variation Tip: Use Canola oil instead of olive oil.
Nutritional Information Per Serving: Calories 1510 | Fat 51.3g| Sodium 525mg | Carbs 163g | Fiber 24.7 g | Sugar 21.4g | Protein 102.9

Cornish Hen with Baked Potatoes

Prep Time: 20 Minutes
Cook Time: 45 Minutes
Serves: 2
Ingredients
- Salt, to taste
- 1 large potato
- 1 tablespoon avocado oil
- 1.5 pounds Cornish hen, skinless and whole
- 2 to 3 teaspoons poultry seasoning, dry rub

Directions
1. Take a fork and pierce the large potato.
2. Rub the potato with avocado oil and salt.
3. Now put the potatoes in the bottom of basket.
4. Now pick the Cornish hen and season the hen with poultry seasoning (dry rub) and salt.
5. Remember to coat the whole Cornish hen well.
6. Now place the hen over the potatoes inside the basket.

7. Now set it to AIR FRY mode at 350 degrees F, for 45 minutes.
8. Once the cooking cycle complete, turn off the air fryer and take out the potatoes and Cornish hen from the air fryer basket.
9. Serve hot and enjoy.
Serving Suggestion: Serve it with Coleslaw.
Variation Tip: You can use olive oil or canola oil instead of avocado oil.
Nutritional Information Per Serving: Calories 612 | Fat14.3 g| Sodium 304mg | Carbs33.4 g | Fiber 4.5 g | Sugar 1.5g | Protein 83.2 g

Chicken Breast Strips

Prep Time: 10 Minutes
Cook Time: 22 Minutes
Serves: 2
Ingredient
- 2 large organic egg
- 1-ounce buttermilk
- 1 cup cornmeal
- ¼ cup all-purpose flour
- Salt and black pepper, to taste
- 1 pound chicken breasts, cut into strips
- 2 tablespoons oil bay seasoning
- oil spray, for greasing

Directions
1. Take a medium bowl and whisk eggs with buttermilk.
2. In a separate large bowl, mix flour, cornmeal, salt, black pepper, and oil bay seasoning.
3. First, dip the chicken breast strip in egg wash and then dredge into the flour mixture.
4. Coat the strip all over and layer it inside the basket that is already grease with oil spray.
5. Grease the chicken breast strips with oil spray as well.
6. Set the basket to AIR FRY mode at 400 degrees F for 22 minutes.
7. Hit the START/PAUSE button to let the cooking start.
8. Once the cooking cycle is done, serve.
Serving Suggestion: Serve it with roasted vegetables.
Variation Tip: None
Nutritional Information Per Serving: Calories 788| Fat25g| Sodium835 mg | Carbs60g | Fiber 4.9g| Sugar1.5g | Protein79g

Cornish Hen with Asparagus

Prep Time: 20 Minutes
Cook Time: 45 Minutes
Serves: 2
Ingredients
- 10 spears asparagus
- Salt and black pepper, to taste
- 1 Cornish hen
- Salt, to taste
- Black pepper, to taste
- 1 teaspoon Paprika
- Coconut spray, for greasing
- 2 lemons, sliced

Directions
1. Wash and pat dry the asparagus and coat it with coconut oil spray.
2. Sprinkle salt on the asparagus and place inside the bottom of the basket of the air fryer.

3. Next, take the Cornish hen and rub it well with the salt, black pepper, and paprika.
4. Oil sprays the Cornish hen and place it on top of asparagus inside the air fryer basket.
5. Set the time to 45 minutes at 350 degrees F, by selecting the ROAST mode.
6. Once the 6 minutes pass hit START/PAUSE button and take out the asparagus.
7. Put the basket back in unit.
8. Once the chicken cooking cycle complete, transfer chicken to the serving plate.
9. Serve the chicken with roasted asparagus and slices of lemon.
10. Serve hot and enjoy.
Serving Suggestion: Serve it with ranch dressing.
Variation Tip: You can add variation by choosing chopped cilantro instead of a lemon slice.
Nutritional Information Per Serving: Calories 192| Fat 4.7g| Sodium 151mg | Carbs10.7 g | Fiber 4.6g | Sugar 3.8g | Protein 30g

2. Soak the chicken thighs and chicken legs in the buttermilk for 2 hours.
3. Mix flour, all the seasonings, and olive oil in a small bowl.
4. Take out the chicken pieces from the buttermilk mixture and then dredge them into the flour mixture.
5. Repeat the steps for all the pieces and then arrange it into the air fryer basket.
6. Set the timer by selecting ROAST mode for 35-40 minutes at 350 degrees F.
7. Once the cooking cycle complete select the pause button and then take out the basket.
8. Serve and enjoy.
Serving Suggestion: Serve the chicken with garlic dipping sauce.
Variation Tip: Use canola oil instead of olive oil.
Nutritional Information Per Serving: Calories 624| Fat17.6 g| Sodium300 mg | Carbs 60g | Fiber 3.5g | Sugar 7.7g | Protein54.2 g

Spicy Chicken

Prep Time: 12 Minutes
Cook Time: 35-40 Minutes
Serves: 4
Ingredients
- 4 chicken thighs
- 2 cups butter milk
- 4 chicken legs
- 2 cups flour
- Salt and black pepper, to taste
- 2 tablespoons garlic powder
- ½ teaspoon onion powder
- 1 teaspoon poultry seasoning
- 1 teaspoon cumin
- 2 tablespoons paprika
- 1 tablespoon olive oil

Directions
1. Take a bowl and add buttermilk to it.

Spice-Rubbed Chicken Pieces

Prep Time: 22 Minutes
Cook Time: 40 Minutes
Serves: 6
Ingredients
- 3 pounds chicken, pieces
- 1 teaspoon sweet paprika
- 1 teaspoon mustard powder
- 1 tablespoon brown sugar, dark
- Salt and black pepper, to taste
- 1 teaspoon Chile powder, New Mexico
- 1 teaspoon oregano, dried
- ¼ teaspoon allspice powder, ground

Directions
1. Take a bowl and mix dark brown sugar, salt, paprika, mustard powder, oregano, Chile powder, black pepper, and all spice powder.
2. Mix well and rub this spice mixture all over the chicken.
3. Put the chicken into the air fryer basket.
4. Oil sprays the chicken from top.

5. Now set the time to 40 minutes at 350 degrees F.
6. Now press START/PAUSE and once the cooking cycle completes, press START/PAUSE.
7. Take out the chicken and serve hot.
Serving Suggestion: Serve it with coleslaw, peanut sauce, or ranch.
Variation Tip: Use light brown sugar instead of dark brown sugar.
Nutritional Information Per Serving: Calories353 | Fat 7.1g| Sodium400 mg | Carbs 2.2g | Fiber0.4 g | Sugar 1.6g | Protein 66g

Chicken Wings

Prep Time: 15 Minutes
Cook Time: 20 Minutes
Serves: 3
Ingredients
- 1 cup chicken batter mix, Louisiana
- 9 Chicken wings
- ½ teaspoon smoked paprika
- 2 tablespoons Dijon mustard
- 1 tablespoon cayenne pepper
- 1 teaspoon meat tenderizer, powder
- Oil spray, for greasing

Directions
1. Pat dry chicken wings, and add mustard, paprika, meat tenderizer, and cayenne pepper.
2. Dredge it in the chicken batter mix.
3. Oil sprays the chicken wings.
4. Grease the basket of the air fryer.
5. Put the wings into the air fryer.
6. Set it to AIR FRY mode at 400 degrees F for 20 minutes
7. Hit START/PAUSE to begin with the cooking.
8. Once the cooking cycle complete, serve, and enjoy hot.
Serving Suggestion: Serve it with salad.

Variation Tip: Use American yellow mustard instead of Dijon mustard.
Nutritional Information Per Serving: Calories621 | Fat 32.6g| Sodium 2016mg | Carbs 46.6g | Fiber 1.1g | Sugar 0.2g | Protein 32.1g

Crumbed Chicken Katsu

Prep Time: 15 minutes.
Cook Time: 26 minutes.
Serves: 4
Ingredients:
- 1 lb. boneless chicken breast, cut in half
- 2 large eggs, beaten
- 1½ cups panko bread crumbs
- Salt and black pepper ground to taste
- Cooking spray

Sauce:
- 1 tablespoon sugar
- 2 tablespoons soy sauce
- 1 tablespoon sherry
- ½ cup ketchup
- 2 teaspoons Worcestershire sauce
- 1 teaspoon garlic, minced

Preparation:
1. At 390 degrees F, preheat your Air Fryer on Air Fry mode.
2. Mix soy sauce, ketchup, sherry, sugar, garlic, and Worcestershire sauce in a mixing bowl.
3. Keep this katsu aside for a while.
4. Rub the chicken pieces with salt and black pepper.
5. Whisk eggs in a shallow dish and spread breadcrumbs in another tray.
6. Dip the chicken in the egg mixture and coat them with breadcrumbs.
7. Place the coated chicken in the Air Fryer Basket and spray them with cooking spray.
8. Return the Air Fryer Basket to the Air Fryer and cook for 26 minutes.
9. Initiate cooking by pressing the START/PAUSE BUTTON.
10. Flip the chicken once cooked halfway through, then resume cooking.

11. Serve warm with the sauce.
Serving Suggestion: Serve with fried rice and green beans salad.
Variation Tip: Coat the chicken with crushed cornflakes for extra crispiness.
Nutritional Information Per Serving:
Calories 220 | Fat 1.7g |Sodium 178mg | Carbs 1.7g | Fiber 0.2g | Sugar 0.2g | Protein 32.9g

Pickled Chicken Fillets

Prep Time: 15 minutes.
Cook Time: 28 minutes.
Serves: 4
Ingredients:
- 2 boneless chicken breasts
- ½ cup dill pickle juice
- 2 eggs
- ½ cup milk
- 1 cup flour, all-purpose
- 2 tablespoons powdered sugar
- 2 tablespoons potato starch
- 1 teaspoon paprika
- 1 teaspoon of sea salt
- ½ teaspoon black pepper
- ½ teaspoon garlic powder
- ¼ teaspoon ground celery seed ground
- 1 tablespoon olive oil
- Cooking spray
- 4 hamburger buns, toasted
- 8 dill pickle chips

Preparation:
1. At 390 degrees F, preheat your Air Fryer on Air Fry mode.
2. Set the chicken in a suitable Ziplock bag and pound it into ½ thickness with a mallet.
3. Slice the chicken into 2 halves.
4. Add pickle juice and seal the bag.
5. Refrigerate for 30 minutes approximately for marination. Whisk both eggs with milk in a shallow bowl.
6. Thoroughly mix flour with spices and flour in a separate bowl.
7. Dip each chicken slice in egg, then in the flour mixture.
8. Shake off the excess and set the chicken pieces in the Air Fryer Basket.
9. Spray the pieces with cooking oil.
10. Place the chicken pieces in the Air Fryer Basket in a single layer and spray the cooking oil.
11. Return the Air Fryer Basket to the Air Fryer and cook for 28 minutes.
12. Initiate cooking by pressing the START/PAUSE BUTTON.
13. Flip the chicken pieces once cooked halfway through, and resume cooking.
14. Enjoy with pickle chips and a dollop of mayonnaise.
Serving Suggestion: Serve with warm corn tortilla and Greek salad.
Variation Tip: You can use the almond flour breading for a low-carb serving.
Nutritional Information Per Serving:
Calories 353 | Fat 5g |Sodium 818mg | Carbs 53.2g | Fiber 4.4g | Sugar 8g | Protein 17.3g

Crusted Chicken Breast

Prep Time: 15 minutes.
Cook Time: 28 minutes.
Serves: 4
Ingredients:
- 2 large eggs, beaten
- ½ cup all-purpose flour
- 1¼ cups panko bread crumbs
- ⅔ cup Parmesan, grated
- 4 teaspoons lemon zest
- 2 teaspoons dried oregano
- Salt, to taste
- 1 teaspoon cayenne pepper
- Freshly black pepper, to taste
- 4 boneless skinless chicken breasts

Preparation:
1. At 390 degrees F, preheat your Air Fryer on Air Fry mode.
2. Beat eggs in one shallow bowl and spread flour in another shallow bowl.

3. Mix panko with oregano, lemon zest, Parmesan, cayenne, oregano, salt, and black pepper in another shallow bowl.
4. First, coat the chicken with flour first, then dip it in the eggs and coat them with panko mixture.
5. Arrange the prepared chicken in the Air Fryer Basket.
6. Return the Air Fryer Basket to the Air Fryer and cook for 28 minutes.
7. Initiate cooking by pressing the START/PAUSE BUTTON.
8. Flip the half-cooked chicken and continue cooking until golden.
9. Serve warm.

Serving Suggestion: Serve with fresh-cut tomatoes and sautéed greens.
Variation Tip: Rub the chicken with lemon juice before seasoning.
Nutritional Information Per Serving:
Calories 220 | Fat 13g |Sodium 542mg | Carbs 0.9g | Fiber 0.3g | Sugar 0.2g | Protein 25.6g

4. Add potato to the chicken and mix well to coat.
5. Spread the mixture in the Air Fryer Basket in a single layer.
6. Return the Air Fryer Basket to the Air Fryer and cook for 22 minutes.
7. Top the chicken and potatoes with cheese and bacon.
8. Return the Air Fryer Basket to the Air Fryer.
9. Select the Air Broil mode with 300 degrees F temperature and 5 minutes cooking time.
10. Initiate cooking by pressing the START/PAUSE BUTTON.
11. Enjoy with dried herbs on top.

Serving Suggestion: Serve with boiled white rice.
Variation Tip: Add sweet potatoes and green beans instead of potatoes.
Nutritional Information Per Serving:
Calories 346 | Fat 16.1g |Sodium 882mg | Carbs 1.3g | Fiber 0.5g | Sugar 0.5g | Protein 48.2g

Chicken Potatoes

Prep Time: 10 minutes.
Cook Time: 22 minutes.
Serves: 4
Ingredients:
- 15 ounces canned potatoes drained
- 1 teaspoon olive oil
- 1 teaspoon Lawry's seasoned salt
- ⅛ teaspoon black pepper optional
- 8 ounces boneless chicken breast cubed
- ¼ teaspoon paprika
- ⅜ cup cheddar, shredded
- 4 bacon slices, cooked, cut into strips

Preparation:
1. At 300 degrees F, preheat your Air Fryer on Air Fry mode.
2. Dice the chicken into small pieces and toss them with olive oil and spices.
3. Drain and dice the potato pieces into smaller cubes.

Chicken Drumettes

Prep Time: 15 minutes.
Cook Time: 52 minutes.
Serves: 5
Ingredients:
- 10 large chicken drumettes
- Cooking spray
- ¼ cup rice vinegar
- 3 tablespoons honey
- 2 tablespoons unsalted chicken stock
- 1 tablespoon soy sauce
- 1 tablespoon toasted sesame oil
- ⅜ teaspoon crushed red pepper
- 1 garlic clove, chopped
- 2 tablespoons chopped unsalted roasted peanuts
- 1 tablespoon chopped fresh chives

Preparation:
1. At 390 degrees F, preheat your Air Fryer on Air Fry mode.

2. Spread the chicken in the Air Fryer Basket in an even layer and spray cooking spray on top.
3. Return the Air Fryer Basket to the Air Fryer and cook for 47 minutes.
4. Initiate cooking by pressing the START/PAUSE BUTTON.
5. Flip the chicken drumettes once cooked halfway through, then resume cooking.
6. During this time, mix soy sauce, honey, stock, vinegar, garlic, and crushed red pepper in a suitable saucepan and place it over medium-high heat to cook on a simmer.
7. Cook this sauce for 6 minutes with occasional stirring, then pour it into a medium-sized bowl.
8. Add Air fried drumettes and toss well to coat with the honey sauce.
9. Garnish with chives and peanuts.
10. Serve warm and fresh.

Serving Suggestion: Serve with tomato ketchup or chili sauce.
Variation Tip: Rub the chicken with lemon juice before seasoning.
Nutritional Information Per Serving:
Calories 268 | Fat 10.4g |Sodium 411mg | Carbs 0.4g | Fiber 0.1g | Sugar 0.1g | Protein 40.6g

Chili Chicken Wings

Prep Time: 20 minutes.
Cook Time: 43 minutes.
Serves: 4
Ingredients:
- 8 chicken wings drumettes
- cooking spray
- ⅛ cup low-fat buttermilk
- ¼ cup almond flour
- McCormick chicken seasoning to taste

Thai Chili Marinade
- 1 ½ tablespoons low-sodium soy sauce
- ½ teaspoon ginger, minced
- 1 ½ garlic cloves
- 1 green onion
- ½ teaspoon rice wine vinegar
- ½ tablespoon Sriracha sauce
- ½ tablespoon sesame oil

Preparation:
1. At 390 degrees F, preheat your Air Fryer on Air Fry mode.
2. Put all the ingredients for the marinade in the blender and blend them for 1 minute.
3. Keep this marinade aside. Pat dry the washed chicken and place it in the Ziploc bag.
4. Add buttermilk, chicken seasoning, and zip the bag.
5. Shake the bag well, then refrigerator for 30 minutes for marination.
6. Remove the chicken drumettes from the marinade, then dredge them through dry flour.
7. Spread the drumettes in the Air Fryer Basket and spray them with cooking oil.
8. Return the Air Fryer Basket to the Air Fryer and cook for 43 minutes.
9. Initiate cooking by pressing the START/PAUSE BUTTON.
10. Toss the drumettes once cooked halfway through.
11. Now brush the chicken pieces with Thai chili sauce and then resume cooking.
12. Serve warm.

Serving Suggestion: Serve with warm corn tortilla and ketchup.
Variation Tip: Rub the wings with lemon or orange juice before cooking.
Nutritional Information Per Serving:
Calories 223 | Fat 11.7g |Sodium 721mg | Carbs 13.6g | Fiber 0.7g | Sugar 8g | Protein 15.7g

Brazilian Chicken Drumsticks

Prep Time: 15 minutes.
Cook Time: 27 minutes.
Serves: 6

Ingredients:
- 2 teaspoons cumin seeds
- 2 teaspoons dried parsley
- 2 teaspoons turmeric powder
- 2 teaspoons dried oregano leaves
- 2 teaspoons salt
- 1 teaspoon coriander seeds
- 1 teaspoon black peppercorns
- 1 teaspoon cayenne pepper
- ½ cup lime juice
- 4 tablespoons vegetable oil
- 3 lbs. chicken drumsticks

Preparation:
1. At 390 degrees F, preheat your Air Fryer on Air Fry mode.
2. Grind cumin, parsley, salt, coriander seeds, cayenne pepper, peppercorns, oregano, and turmeric in a food processor.
3. Add this mixture to lemon juice and oil in a bowl and mix well.
4. Rub the spice paste over the chicken drumsticks and let them marinate for 30 minutes.
5. Place the chicken drumsticks in the Air Fryer Basket.
6. Return the Air Fryer Basket to the Air Fryer and cook for 27 minutes.
7. Initiate cooking by pressing the START/PAUSE BUTTON.
8. Flip the drumsticks when cooked halfway through, then resume cooking.
9. Serve warm.

Serving Suggestion: Serve with tomato ketchup or chili sauce.

Variation Tip: Use buttermilk to soak the drumsticks before seasoning.

Nutritional Information Per Serving:
Calories 456 | Fat 16.4g | Sodium 1321mg | Carbs 19.2g | Fiber 2.2g | Sugar 4.2g | Protein 55.2g

Bang-Bang Chicken

Prep Time: 15 minutes.
Cook Time: 20 minutes.
Serves: 2

Ingredients:
- 1 cup mayonnaise
- ½ cup sweet chili sauce
- 2 tablespoons Sriracha sauce
- ⅓ cup flour
- 1 lb. boneless chicken breast, diced
- 1½ cups panko bread crumbs
- 2 green onions, chopped

Preparation:
1. At 390 degrees F, preheat your Air Fryer on Air Fry mode.
2. Mix mayonnaise with Sriracha and sweet chili sauce in a large bowl.
3. Keep ¾ cup of the mixture aside.
4. Add flour, chicken, breadcrumbs, and remaining mayo mixture to a resealable plastic bag.
5. Zip the bag and shake well to coat.
6. Place the chicken in the Air Fryer Basket in a single layer.
7. Return the Air Fryer Basket to the Air Fryer and cook for 20 minutes.
8. Initiate cooking by pressing the START/PAUSE BUTTON.
9. Flip the chicken once cooked halfway through.

10. Top the chicken with reserved mayo sauce.
11. Garnish with green onions and serve warm.
Serving Suggestion: Serve with tomato ketchup or chili sauce.
Variation Tip: Use crushed cornflakes for breading to have extra crispiness.
Nutritional Information Per Serving:
Calories 374 | Fat 13g | Sodium 552mg | Carbs 25g | Fiber 1.2g | Sugar 1.2g | Protein 37.7g

Veggie Stuffed Chicken Breasts

Prep Time: 15 minutes.
Cook Time: 10 minutes.
Serves: 2
Ingredients:
- 4 teaspoons chili powder
- 4 teaspoons ground cumin
- 1 skinless, boneless chicken breast
- 2 teaspoons chipotle flakes
- 2 teaspoons Mexican oregano
- Salt and black pepper, to taste
- ½ red bell pepper, julienned
- ½ onion, julienned
- 1 fresh jalapeno pepper, julienned
- 2 teaspoons corn oil
- ½ lime, juiced

Preparation:
1. At 360 degrees F, preheat your Air Fryer on Air Fry mode.
2. Slice the chicken breast in half horizontally.
3. Pound each chicken breast with a mallet into ¼-inch thickness.
4. Rub the pounded chicken breast with black pepper, salt, oregano, chipotle flakes, cumin, and chili powder.
5. Add ½ of bell pepper, jalapeno, and onion on top of each chicken breast piece.
6. Roll the chicken to wrap the filling inside and insert toothpicks to seal.
7. Place the rolls in the Air Fryer Basket and spray them with cooking oil.
8. Return the Air Fryer Basket to the Air Fryer and cook for 10 minutes.
9. Initiate cooking by pressing the START/PAUSE BUTTON.
10. Serve warm.
Serving Suggestion: Serve with tomato ketchup or chili sauce.
Variation Tip: Season the chicken rolls with seasoned parmesan before cooking.
Nutritional Information Per Serving:
Calories 351 | Fat 11g | Sodium 150mg | Carbs 3.3g | Fiber 0.2g | Sugar 1g | Protein 33.2g

General Tso's Chicken

Prep Time: 20 minutes.
Cook Time: 22 minutes.
Serves: 4
Ingredients:
- 1 egg, large
- ⅓ cup 2 teaspoons cornstarch,
- ¼ teaspoon salt
- ¼ teaspoon ground white pepper
- 7 tablespoons chicken broth
- 2 tablespoons soy sauce
- 2 tablespoons ketchup
- 2 teaspoons sugar
- 2 teaspoons unseasoned rice vinegar
- 1 ½ tablespoons canola oil
- 4 chilies de árbol, chopped and seeds discarded
- 1 tablespoon chopped fresh ginger
- 1 tablespoon garlic, chopped
- 2 tablespoons green onion, sliced
- 1 teaspoon toasted sesame oil
- 1 lb. boneless chicken thighs, cut into 1 ¼ - inch chunks
- ½ teaspoon toasted sesame seeds

Preparation:
1. At 390 degrees F, preheat your Air Fryer on Air Fry mode.

2. Add egg to a large bowl and beat it with a fork.
3. Add chicken to the egg and coat it well.
4. Whisk ⅓ cup of cornstarch with black pepper and salt in a small bowl.
5. Add chicken to the cornstarch mixture and mix well to coat.
6. Place the chicken in the Air Fryer Basket and spray them with cooking oil.
7. Return the Air Fryer Basket to the Air Fryer and cook for 20 minutes.
8. Initiate cooking by pressing the START/PAUSE BUTTON.
9. Once done, remove the air fried chicken from the Air fryer.
10. Whisk 2 teaspoons of cornstarch with soy sauce, broth, sugar, ketchup, and rice vinegar in a small bowl.
11. Add chilies and canola oil to a skillet and sauté for 1 minute.
12. Add garlic and ginger, then sauté for 30 seconds.
13. Stir in cornstarch sauce and cook until it bubbles and thickens.
14. Toss in cooked chicken and garnish with sesame oil, sesame seeds, and green onion.
15. Enjoy.

Serving Suggestion: Serve with boiled white rice or chow Mein.
Variation Tip: You can use honey instead of sugar to sweeten the sauce.
Nutritional Information Per Serving:
Calories 351 | Fat 16g |Sodium 777mg | Carbs 26g | Fiber 4g | Sugar 5g | Protein 28g

Bacon-Wrapped Chicken

Prep Time: 10 minutes.
Cook Time: 28 minutes.
Serves: 2
Ingredients:
- Butter:
- ½ stick butter softened
- ½ garlic clove, minced
- ¼ teaspoons dried thyme
- ¼ teaspoons dried basil
- ⅛ teaspoons coarse salt
- 1 pinch black pepper, ground
- ⅓ lb. thick-cut bacon
- 1 ½ lbs. boneless skinless chicken thighs
- 2 teaspoons garlic, minced

Preparation:
1. At 390 degrees F, preheat your Air Fryer on Air Fry mode.
2. Mix garlic softened butter with thyme, salt, basil, and black pepper in a bowl.
3. Add butter mixture on a piece of wax paper and roll it up tightly to make a butter log.
4. Place the log in the refrigerator for 2 hours.
5. Spray one bacon strip on a piece of wax paper.
6. Place each chicken thigh on top of one bacon strip and rub it with garlic.
7. Make a slit in the chicken thigh and add a teaspoon of butter to the chicken.
8. Wrap the bacon around the chicken thigh.
9. Repeat those same steps with all the chicken thighs.
10. Place the bacon-wrapped chicken thighs in the Air Fryer Basket.
11. Return the Air Fryer Basket to the Air Fryer and cook for 28 minutes.
12. Initiate cooking by pressing the START/PAUSE BUTTON.
13. Flip the chicken once cooked halfway through, and resume cooking.
14. Serve warm.

Serving Suggestion: Serve with tomato ketchup or chili sauce.
Variation Tip: Drizzle mixed dried herbs on top before cooking.
Nutritional Information Per Serving:
Calories 380 | Fat 29g |Sodium 821mg | Carbs 34.6g | Fiber 0g | Sugar 0g | Protein 30g

Air Fried Turkey Breast

Prep Time: 10 minutes.
Cook Time: 46 minutes.
Serves: 4
Ingredients:
- 2 lbs. turkey breast, on the bone with skin
- ½ tablespoon olive oil
- 1 teaspoon salt
- ¼ tablespoon dry poultry seasoning

Preparation:
1. At 390 degrees F, preheat your Air Fryer on Air Fry mode.
2. Rub turkey breast with ½ tablespoon of oil.
3. Season both its sides with turkey seasoning and salt, then rub in the brush half tablespoon of oil over the skin of the turkey.
4. Place the turkey in the Air Fryer Basket.
5. Return the Air Fryer Basket to the Air Fryer and cook for 46 minutes.
6. Initiate cooking by pressing the START/PAUSE BUTTON.
7. Flip the turkey once cooked halfway through, and resume cooking.
8. Slice and serve warm.

Serving Suggestion: Serve with warm corn tortilla and Greek salad.
Variation Tip: Coat and dust the turkey breast with flour after seasoning.
Nutritional Information Per Serving:
Calories 502 | Fat 25g |Sodium 230mg | Carbs 1.5g | Fiber 0.2g | Sugar 0.4g | Protein 64.1g

Cheddar-Stuffed Chicken

Prep Time: 10 minutes.
Cook Time: 20 minutes.
Serves: 4
Ingredients:
- 3 bacon strips, cooked and crumbled
- 2 ounces Cheddar cheese, cubed
- ¼ cup barbeque sauce
- 2 (4 ounces) boneless chicken breasts
- Salt and black pepper to taste

Preparation:
1. At 360 degrees F, preheat your Air Fryer on Air Fry mode.
2. Make a 1-inch deep pouch in each chicken breast.
3. Mix cheddar cubes with half of the BBQ sauce, salt, black pepper, and bacon.
4. Divide this filling in the chicken breasts and secure the edges with a toothpick.
5. Brush the remaining BBQ sauce over the chicken breasts.
6. Place the chicken in the Air Fryer Basket and spray them with cooking oil.
7. Return the Air Fryer Basket to the Air Fryer and cook for 20 minutes.
8. Initiate cooking by pressing the START/PAUSE BUTTON.
9. Serve warm.

Serving Suggestion: Serve with tomato salsa on top.
Variation Tip: Use poultry seasoning for breading.
Nutritional Information Per Serving:
Calories 379 | Fat 19g |Sodium 184mg | Carbs 12.3g | Fiber 0.6g | Sugar 2g | Protein 37.7g

Chapter 6-Seafood and Fish Recipes

Seafood Shrimp Omelet

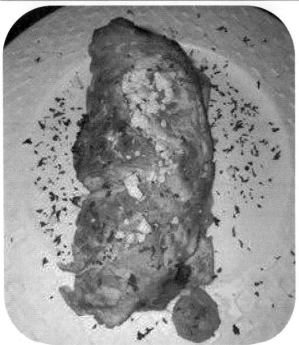

Prep Time: 20 Minutes
Cook Time: 15 Minutes
Serves: 2

Ingredient
- 6 large shrimp, shells removed and chopped
- 6 eggs, beaten
- ½ tablespoon butter, melted
- 2 tablespoons green onions, sliced
- ⅓ cup mushrooms, chopped
- 1 pinch paprika
- Salt and black pepper, to taste
- Oil spray, for greasing

Directions
1. In a large bowl, whisk the eggs and add chopped shrimp, butter, green onions, mushrooms, paprika, salt, and black pepper.
2. Take a cake pan that fit inside the air fryer and grease them with oil spray.
3. Pour the egg mixture in the cake pan and place it inside the basket of the air fryer.
4. Turn on the Air Fry function, and let it cook for 15 minutes at 320 degrees F.
5. Once the cooking cycle completes, take out, and serve hot.

Serving Suggestion: Serve it with rice.
Variation Tip: Use olive oil for greasing purposes.
Nutritional Information Per Serving: Calories 300 | Fat 17.5g| Sodium 368mg | Carbs 2.9g | Fiber 0.3g | Sugar1.4 g | Protein32.2 g

Salmon with Broccoli and Cheese

Prep Time: 15 Minutes
Cook Time: 15 Minutes
Serves: 2

Ingredients
- 2 cups broccoli
- ½ cup butter, melted
- Salt and pepper, to taste
- Oil spray, for greasing
- 1 cup grated cheddar cheese
- 1 pound salmon, fillets

Directions
1. Take a bowl and add broccoli to it.
2. Add salt and black pepper and spray it with oil.
3. Put the broccoli in the basket.
4. Now rub the salmon fillets with salt, black pepper, and butter.
5. Put fish and broccoli inside the basket.
6. Then insert the basket into the unit.
7. Set it to AIR FRY mode for 15 minutes at 400 degrees F.
8. Hit START/PAUSE to start the cooking.
9. Once done, serve by placing it on serving plates.
10. Put the grated cheese on top of the salmon, enjoy.

Serving Suggestion: Serve it with rice and baked potato.
Variation Tip: Use olive oil instead of butter.
Nutritional Information Per Serving: Calories 966 | Fat 79.1 g| Sodium 808 mg | Carbs 6.8 g | Fiber 2.4g | Sugar 1.9g | Protein 61.2 g

Salmon with Green Beans

Prep Time: 12 Minutes
Cook Time: 18 Minutes
Serves: 1 Serving
Ingredients
- 1 salmon fillet, 2 inches thick
- 2 teaspoons olive oil
- 2 teaspoons smoked paprika
- Salt and black pepper, to taste
- 1 cup green beans
- Oil spray, for greasing

Directions
1. Grease the green beans with oil spray and set aside for further use,
2. Now rub the salmon fillet with olive oil, smoked paprika, salt, and black pepper.
3. Put the salmon fillets in the basket of air fryer along with green beans.
4. You can adjust the green beans on a rack as well.
5. Now set it to AIR FRY mode at 350 degrees F for 18 minutes.
6. Once done, take out the salmon and green beans and transfer them to the serving plates and enjoy.

Serving Suggestion: Serve it with ranch dressing.
Variation Tip: Use any other green vegetable of your choice.
Nutritional Information Per Serving: Calories 367| Fat 22g| Sodium 87mg | Carbs 10.2g | Fiber 5.3g | Sugar 2g | Protein 37.2g

Fish and Chips

Prep Time: 15 Minutes
Cook Time: 22 Minutes
Serves: 2
Ingredients
- 1 pound potatoes, cut lengthwise
- 1 cup seasoned flour
- 2 eggs, organic
- ⅓ cup buttermilk
- 2 cup seafood fry mix
- ½ cup bread crumbs
- 2 codfish fillet, 6 ounces each
- Oil spray, for greasing

Directions
1. Take a bowl and whisk eggs in it along buttermilk.
2. In a separate bowl, mix seafood fry mix and bread crumbs
3. Take a baking tray and spread flour on it.
4. Dip the fillets first in egg wash, then in flour, and at the end coat it with breadcrumbs mixture.
5. Put the fish fillet in air fryer basket.
6. Grease the fish fillet with oil spray.
7. Put potato chips inside the basket and lightly grease it with oil spray.
8. Set the air fryer to AIR FRY mode at 400 degrees F for 22 minutes.
9. After 12 minutes take out the fish and continue with the cooking cycle.
10. Once done, serve and enjoy.

Serving Suggestion: Serve it with mayonnaise.
Variation Tip: Use water instead of buttermilk.
Nutritional Information Per Serving: Calories 992| Fat 22.3g| Sodium1406 mg | Carbs 153.6g | Fiber 10g | Sugar 10g | Protein 40g

Codfish with Herb Vinaigrette

Prep Time: 15 Minutes
Cook Time: 16 Minutes
Serves: 2

Ingredients
Vinaigrette Ingredients
- ½ cup parsley leaves
- 1 cup basil leaves
- ½ cup mint leaves
- 2 tablespoons thyme leaves
- ¼ teaspoon red pepper flakes
- 2 cloves garlic
- 4 tablespoons red wine vinegar
- ¼ cup olive oil
- Salt, to taste

Other Ingredients
- 1.5 pounds fish fillets, cod fish
- 2 tablespoons olive oil
- Salt and black pepper, to taste
- 1 teaspoon paprika
- 1 teaspoon Italian seasoning

Directions
1. Blend the entire vinaigrette ingredient in a high-speed blender and pulse into a smooth paste.
2. Set aside for drizzling overcooked fish.
3. Rub the fillets with salt, black pepper, paprika, Italian seasoning, and olive oil. Put it to the basket of the air fryer.
4. Set it to 16 minutes at 390 degrees F, on AIR FRY mode.
5. Once done, serve the fillets with the drizzle of blended vinaigrette.

Serving Suggestion: Serve it with rice.
Variation Tip: Use sour cream instead of cream cheese.
Nutritional Information Per Serving: Calories 1219| Fat 81.8g| Sodium 1906mg | Carbs 64.4g | Fiber 5.5g | Sugar 0.4g | Protein 52.1g

Spicy Fish Fillet with Onion Rings

Prep Time: 10 Minutes
Cook Time: 15 Minutes
Serves: 1 Serving

Ingredients
- 300 grams onion rings, frozen and packed
- 1 codfish fillet, 8 ounces
- Salt and black pepper, to taste
- 1 teaspoon lemon juice
- oil spray, for greasing

Directions
1. Pat dry the fish fillets with a paper towel and season them with salt, black pepper, and lemon juice.
2. Grease the fillet with oil spray.
3. Put the fish in air fryer basket; adjust the onions rings besides.
4. Insert the basket into the unit.
5. Use AIR FRY mode at 350 degrees for 15 minutes.
6. Once done, serve hot.

Serving Suggestion: Serve with buffalo sauce.
Variation Tip: None.
Nutritional Information Per Serving: Calories 666| Fat23.5g| Sodium 911mg | Carbs 82g | Fiber 8.8g | Sugar 17.4g | Protein 30.4g

Beer Battered Fish Fillet

Prep Time: 18 Minutes
Cook Time: 14 Minutes
Serves: 2

Ingredients
- 1 cup all-purpose flour
- 4 tablespoons cornstarch
- 1 teaspoon baking soda
- 8 ounces beer
- 2 egg beaten
- ½ cup all-purpose flour
- 1 teaspoon smoked paprika
- 1 teaspoon salt
- ¼ teaspoon freshly ground black pepper
- ¼ teaspoon cayenne pepper
- 2 cod fillets, 1½-inches thick, cut into 4 pieces
- Oil spray, for greasing

Directions
1. Take a large bowl and combine flour, baking soda, corn starch, and salt.
2. In a separate bowl, beat eggs along with the beer.
3. In a shallow dish, mix paprika, salt, pepper, and cayenne pepper.
4. Dry the codfish fillets with a paper towel.
5. Dip the fish into the eggs and coat it with seasoned flour.
6. Then dip it in the seasoning.
7. Grease the fillet with oil spray.
8. Put the fillets in air fryer basket.
9. Set it to AIR FRY mode at 400 degrees F for 14 minutes.
10. Press START/PAUSE and let the air fryer do its magic.
11. Once cooking is done, serve the fish.
12. Enjoy it hot.

Serving Suggestion: Serve it with rice.
Variation Tip: Use mild paprika instead of smoked paprika.
Nutritional Information Per Serving: Calories 1691| Fat 6.1g| Sodium 3976mg | Carbs105.1 g | Fiber 3.4g | Sugar15.6 g | Protein 270g

Keto Baked Salmon with Pesto

Prep Time: 15 Minutes
Cook Time: 18 Minutes
Serves: 2

Ingredients
- 4 salmon fillets, 2 inches thick
- 2 ounces green pesto
- Salt and black pepper
- ½ tablespoon canola oil, for greasing

Ingredients for Green Sauce
- 1-½ cup mayonnaise
- 2 tablespoons Greek yogurt
- Salt and black pepper, to taste

Directions
1. Rub the salmon with pesto, salt, oil, and black pepper.
2. In a small bowl, whisk together all the green sauce ingredients.
3. Put the fish fillets in the basket.
4. Set the AIR FRY mode for 18 minutes at 390 degrees F.
5. Once the cooking is done, serve it with green sauce drizzle.
6. Enjoy.

Serving Suggestion: Serve it with mashed cheesy potatoes.
Variation Tip: Use butter instead of canal oil.
Nutritional Information Per Serving: Calories 1165 | Fat80.7 g| Sodium 1087 mg | Carbs 33.1g | Fiber 0.5g | Sugar11.5 g | Protein 80.6g

Smoked Salmon

Prep Time: 20 Minutes
Cook Time: 12 Minutes
Serves: 4

Ingredients
- 2 pounds salmon fillets, smoked
- 6 ounces cream cheese
- 4 tablespoons mayonnaise
- 2 teaspoons chives, fresh
- 1 teaspoon lemon zest
- Salt and freshly ground black pepper, to taste
- 2 tablespoons butter

Directions
1. Cut the salmon into very small and uniform bite-size pieces.
2. Mix cream cheese, chives, mayonnaise, black pepper, and lemon zest, in a small mixing bowl.
3. Let it sit aside for further use.
4. Coat the salmon pieces with salt and butter.
5. Put it into the basket of the air fryer.
6. Set it on AIR FRY mode at 400 degrees F for 12 minutes.
7. Hit START/PAUSE, so the cooking starts.
8. Once the salmon is done, top it with a bowl creamy mixture and serve.
9. Enjoy hot.

Serving Suggestion: Serve it with rice.
Variation Tip: Use sour cream instead of cream cheese.
Nutritional Information Per Serving: Calories 557| Fat 15.7 g| Sodium 371mg | Carbs 4.8 g | Fiber 0g | Sugar 1.1g | Protein 48 g

Two-Way Salmon

Prep Time: 10 Minutes
Cook Time: 18 Minutes
Serves: 2

Ingredients
- 2 salmon fillets, 8 ounces each
- 2 tablespoons Cajun seasoning
- 2 tablespoons jerk seasoning
- 1 lemon cut in half
- Oil spray, for greasing

Directions
1. First, drizzle lemon juice over the salmon and wash it with tap water.
2. Rinse and pat dry the fillets with a paper towel.
3. Now rub o fillet with Cajun seasoning and grease it with oil spray.
4. Take the second fillet and rub it with jerk seasoning.
5. Grease the second fillet of salmon with oil spray.
6. Now put the salmon fillets in the air fryer basket.
7. Set the basket to 390 degrees F for 16-18 minutes at AIR FRY mode.
8. Hit the START/PAUSE button to start cooking.
9. Once the cooking is done, serve the fish fillets hot with mayonnaise.

Serving Suggestion: Serve it with ranch.
Variation Tip: None.
Nutritional Information Per Serving: Calories 238| Fat 11.8g| Sodium 488mg | Carbs 9g | Fiber 0g | Sugar 8g | Protein 35g

Lemon Pepper Salmon with Asparagus

Prep Time: 20 Minutes
Cook Time: 20 Minutes
Serves: 2

Ingredients
- 1 cup green asparagus
- 2 tablespoons butter
- 2 fillets salmon, 8 ounces each
- Salt and black pepper, to taste
- 1 teaspoon lemon juice
- ½ teaspoon lemon zest
- oil spray, for greasing

Directions
1. Rinse and trim the asparagus.
2. Rinse and pat dry the salmon fillets.
3. Take a bowl and mix lemon juice, lemon zest, salt, and black pepper.
4. Brush the fish fillet with the rub and place it in the basket along with asparagus.
5. Set it to AIR FRY mode for 20 minutes at 390 degrees F.
6. Once 5 minutes passes, take out the basket and remove asparagus.
7. Continue with the cooking cycle.
8. Once done, serve and enjoy.

Serving Suggestion: Serve it with baked potato.
Variation Tip: Use olive oil instead of butter.
Nutritional Information Per Serving: Calories 482| Fat 28g| Sodium 209 mg | Carbs 2.8g | Fiber 1.5 g | Sugar 1.4 g | Protein 56.3g

Salmon with Coconut

Prep Time: 10 Minutes
Cook Time: 12 Minutes
Serves: 2

Ingredients
- Oil spray, for greasing
- 2 salmon fillets, 6 ounces each
- Salt and ground black pepper, to taste
- 1 tablespoon butter, for frying
- 1 tablespoon red curry paste
- 1 cup of coconut cream
- 2 tablespoons fresh cilantro, chopped
- 1 cup cauliflower florets
- ½ cup Parmesan cheese, hard

Directions
1. Take a bowl and mix salt, black pepper, butter, red curry paste, coconut cream in a bowl and marinate the salmon in it.
2. Oil sprays the cauliflower florets and then seasons it with salt and freshly ground black pepper.
3. Put the florets in the air fryer basket and then place the salmon fillet aside.
4. Set it to AIR FRY mode at 12 minutes for 400 degrees F.
5. Once the time for cooking is over, serve the salmon with cauliflower floret with Parmesan cheese drizzle on top.

Serving Suggestion: Serve it with rice.
Variation Tip: Use mozzarella cheese instead of Parmesan cheese.
Nutritional Information Per Serving: Calories 774 | Fat 59g| Sodium 1223mg | Carbs 12.2g | Fiber 3.9g | Sugar 5.9g | Protein 53.5g

Frozen Breaded Fish Fillet

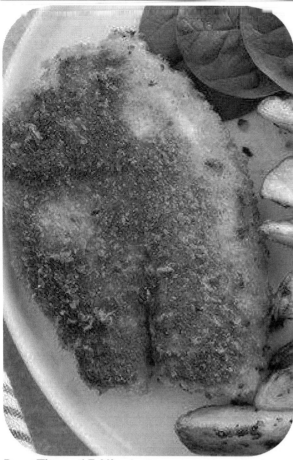

Prep Time: 15 Minutes
Cook Time: 12 Minutes
Serves: 2
Ingredients
- 4 frozen breaded fish fillet
- Oil spray, for greasing
- 1 cup mayonnaise

Directions
1. Take the frozen fish fillets out of the bag and place them in the basket of the air fryer.
2. Lightly grease it with oil spray.
3. Set the unit to 380 degrees F for 12 minutes at AIR FRY mode.
4. Hit the START/PAUSE button to start cooking.
5. Once the cooking is done, serve the fish hot with mayonnaise.

Serving Suggestion: Serve it with salad and rice.
Variation Tip: Use olive oil instead of butter.
Nutritional Information per Serving: Calories 921| Fat 61.5g| Sodium 1575mg | Carbs 69g | Fiber 2g | Sugar 9.5g | Protein 29.1g

Salmon Nuggets

Prep Time: 15 minutes.
Cook Time: 15 minutes.
Serves: 4
Ingredients:
- ⅓ cup maple syrup
- ¼ teaspoon dried chipotle pepper
- 1 pinch sea salt
- 1 ½ cups croutons
- 1 large egg
- 1 (1 pound) skinless salmon fillet, cut into 1 ½-inch chunk
- cooking spray

Preparation:
1. At 390 degrees F, preheat your Air Fryer on Air Fry mode.
2. Mix chipotle powder, maple syrup, and salt in a saucepan and cook on a simmer for 5 minutes.
3. Crush the croutons in a food processor and transfer them to a bowl.
4. Beat egg in another shallow bowl.
5. Season the salmon chunks with sea salt.
6. Dip the salmon in the egg, then coat with breadcrumbs.
7. Spread the coated salmon chunks in the Air Fryer Basket.
8. Return the Air Fryer Basket to the Air Fryer and cook for 10 minutes.
9. Initiate cooking by pressing the START/PAUSE BUTTON.
10. Flip the chunks once cooked halfway through, then resume cooking.
11. Pour the maple syrup on top and serve warm.

Serving Suggestion: Serve with creamy dip and crispy fries.
Variation Tip: Use crushed cornflakes for breading to have extra crispiness.
Nutritional Information Per Serving:
Calories 275 | Fat 1.4g |Sodium 582mg | Carbs 31.5g | Fiber 1.1g | Sugar 0.1g | Protein 29.8g

Fish Sandwich

Prep Time: 15 minutes.
Cook Time: 22 minutes.
Serves: 4

Ingredients:
- 4 small cod fillets, skinless
- Salt and black pepper, to taste
- 2 tablespoons flour
- ¼ cup dried breadcrumbs
- Spray oil
- 9 ounces frozen peas
- 1 tablespoon creme fraiche
- 12 capers
- 1 squeeze lemon juice
- 4 bread rolls, cut in halve

Preparation:
1. At 390 degrees F, preheat your Air Fryer on Air Fry mode.
2. First, coat the cod fillets with flour, salt, and black pepper.
3. Then coat the fish with breadcrumbs.
4. Place the coated codfish in the Air Fryer Basket and spray them with cooking spray.
5. Return the Air Fryer Basket to the Air Fryer and cook for 17 minutes.
6. Initiate cooking by pressing the START/PAUSE BUTTON.
7. Meanwhile, boil peas in hot water for 5 minutes until soft.
8. Then drain the peas and transfer them to the blender.
9. Add capers, lemon juice, and crème fraiche to the blender.
10. Blend until it makes a smooth mixture.
11. Spread the peas crème mixture on top of 2 lower halves of the bread roll, and place the fish fillets on it.
12. Place the remaining bread slices on top.
13. Serve fresh.

Serving Suggestion: Serve with sautéed or fresh greens with melted butter.

Variation Tip: Coat the fish with crushed cornflakes for extra crispiness.

Nutritional Information Per Serving:
Calories 348 | Fat 30g |Sodium 660mg | Carbs 5g | Fiber 0g | Sugar 0g | Protein 14g

Breaded Scallops

Prep Time: 15 minutes.
Cook Time: 12 minutes.
Serves: 4

Ingredients:
- ½ cup crushed buttery crackers
- ½ teaspoon garlic powder
- ½ teaspoon seafood seasoning
- 2 tablespoons butter, melted
- 1-pound sea scallops patted dry
- cooking spray

Preparation:
1. At 390 degrees F, preheat your Air Fryer on Air Fry mode.
2. Mix cracker crumbs, garlic powder, and seafood seasoning in a shallow bowl. Spread melted butter in another shallow bowl.
3. Dip each scallop in the melted butter and then roll in the breading to coat well.
4. Grease the Air Fryer Basket with cooking spray and place the scallops inside.
5. Return the Air Fryer Basket to the Air Fryer and cook for 12 minutes.
6. Initiate cooking by pressing the START/PAUSE BUTTON.
7. Flip the scallops with a spatula after 4 minutes and resume cooking.
8. Serve warm.

Serving Suggestion: Serve with creamy dip and crispy fries.

Variation Tip: Use crushed cornflakes for breading to have extra crispiness.

Nutritional Information Per Serving:
Calories 275 | Fat 1.4g |Sodium 582mg | Carbs 31.5g | Fiber 1.1g | Sugar 0.1g | Protein 29.8g

Salmon Patties

Prep Time: 15 minutes.
Cook Time: 18 minutes.
Serves: 8

Ingredients:
- 1 lb. fresh Atlantic salmon side
- ¼ cup avocado, mashed
- ¼ cup cilantro, diced
- 1 ½ teaspoons yellow curry powder
- ½ teaspoons sea salt
- ¼ cup, 4 teaspoons tapioca starch
- 2 brown eggs
- ½ cup coconut flakes
- Coconut oil, melted, for brushing

For the greens:
- 2 teaspoons organic coconut oil, melted
- 6 cups arugula & spinach mix, tightly packed
- Pinch of sea salt

Preparation:
1. At 390 degrees F, preheat your Air Fryer on Air Fry mode.
2. Remove the fish skin and dice the flesh.
3. Place in a large bowl. Add cilantro, avocado, salt, and curry powder mix gently.
4. Add tapioca starch and mix well again.
5. Make 8 salmon patties out of this mixture, about a half-inch thick.
6. Place them on a baking sheet lined with wax paper and freeze them for 20 minutes.
7. Place ¼ cup of tapioca starch and coconut flakes on a flat plate.
8. Dip the patties in the whisked egg, then coat the frozen patties in the starch and flakes.
9. Place the patties in the Air Fryer Basket and spray them with cooking oil.
10. Return the Air Fryer Basket to the Air Fryer and cook for 17 minutes.
11. Initiate cooking by pressing the START/PAUSE BUTTON.
12. Flip the patties once cooked halfway through, then resume cooking.
13. Sauté arugula with spinach in coconut oil in a pan for 30 seconds.
14. Serve the patties with sautéed greens mixture.

Serving Suggestion: Serve with sautéed green beans or asparagus.
Variation Tip: Add lemon juice to the mixture before mixing.
Nutritional Information Per Serving:
Calories 260 | Fat 16g |Sodium 585mg | Carbs 3.1g | Fiber 1.3g | Sugar 0.2g | Protein 25.5g

Glazed Scallops

Prep Time: 15 minutes.
Cook Time: 13 minutes.
Serves: 6

Ingredients:
- 12 scallops
- 3 tablespoons olive oil
- Black pepper and salt to taste

Preparation:
1. At 390 degrees F, preheat your Air Fryer on Air Fry mode.
2. Rub the scallops with olive oil, black pepper, and salt.
3. Place the scallops in the Air Fryer Basket.
4. Return the Air Fryer Basket to the Air Fryer and cook for 13 minutes.
5. Initiate cooking by pressing the START/PAUSE BUTTON.
6. Flip the scallops once cooked halfway through, and resume cooking.
7. Serve warm.

Serving Suggestion: Serve with melted butter on top.
Variation Tip: Drizzle breadcrumbs on top before air frying.
Nutritional Information Per Serving:
Calories 308 | Fat 24g |Sodium 715mg | Carbs 0.8g | Fiber 0.1g | Sugar 0.1g | Protein 21.9g

Salmon with Fennel Salad

Prep Time: 10 minutes.
Cook Time: 17 minutes.
Serves: 4
Ingredients:
- 2 teaspoons fresh parsley, chopped
- 1 teaspoon fresh thyme, chopped
- 1 teaspoon salt
- 4 (6-oz) skinless center-cut salmon fillets
- 2 tablespoons olive oil
- 4 cups fennel, sliced
- ⅔ cup Greek yogurt
- 1 garlic clove, grated
- 2 tablespoons orange juice
- 1 teaspoon lemon juice
- 2 tablespoons fresh dill, chopped

Preparation:
1. At 390 degrees F, preheat your Air Fryer on Air Fry mode.
2. Mix ½ teaspoon of salt, thyme, and parsley in a small bowl.
3. Brush the salmon with oil first, then rub liberally rub the herb mixture.
4. Place salmon fillets in the Air Fryer Basket.
5. Return the Air Fryer Basket to the Air Fryer and cook for 17 minutes.
6. Initiate cooking by pressing the START/PAUSE BUTTON.
7. Meanwhile, mix fennel with garlic, yogurt, lemon juice, orange juice, remaining salt, and dill in a mixing bowl.
8. Serve the air fried salmon fillets with fennel salad.
9. Enjoy.

Serving Suggestion: Serve with melted butter on top.
Variation Tip: Rub the salmon with lemon juice before cooking.
Nutritional Information Per Serving:
Calories 305 | Fat 15g | Sodium 482mg | Carbs 17g | Fiber 3g | Sugar 2g | Protein 35g

Crusted Tilapia

Prep Time: 20 minutes.
Cook Time: 17 minutes.
Serves: 4
Ingredients:
- ¾ cup breadcrumbs
- 1 packet dry ranch-style dressing
- 2 ½ tablespoons vegetable oil
- 2 eggs beaten
- 4 tilapia fillets
- Herbs and chilies to garnish

Preparation:
1. At 390 degrees F, preheat your Air Fryer on Air Fry mode.
2. Thoroughly mix ranch dressing with panko in a bowl.
3. Whisk eggs in a shallow bowl.
4. Dip each fish fillet in the egg, then coat evenly with the panko mixture.
5. Set two coated fillets in the Air Fryer Basket.
6. Return the Air Fryer Basket to the Air Fryer and cook for 17 minutes.
7. Initiate cooking by pressing the START/PAUSE BUTTON.
8. Serve warm with herbs and chilies

Serving Suggestion: Serve with sautéed asparagus on the side.
Variation Tip: Coat the fish with crushed cornflakes for extra crispiness.
Nutritional Information Per Serving:
Calories 196 | Fat 7.1g | Sodium 492mg | Carbs 21.6g | Fiber 2.9g | Sugar 0.8g | Protein 13.4g

Scallops with Greens

Prep Time: 15 minutes.
Cook Time: 13 minutes.
Serves: 8

Ingredients:
- ¾ cup heavy whipping cream
- 1 tablespoon tomato paste
- 1 tablespoon chopped fresh basil
- 1 teaspoon garlic, minced
- ½ teaspoon salt
- ½ teaspoon pepper
- 12 ounces frozen spinach thawed
- 8 jumbo sea scallops
- Vegetable oil to spray

Preparation:
1. At 390 degrees F, preheat your Air Fryer on Air Fry mode.
2. Season the scallops with vegetable oil, salt, and pepper in a bowl.
3. Mix cream with spinach, basil, garlic, salt, pepper, and tomato paste in a bowl.
4. Pour this mixture over the scallops and mix gently.
5. Place the scallops in the Air Fryers Basket without using the crisper plate.
6. Return the Air Fryer Basket to the Air Fryer and cook for 13 minutes.
7. Initiate cooking by pressing the START/PAUSE BUTTON.
8. Serve right away.

Serving Suggestion: Serve with fresh cucumber salad.
Variation Tip: Use crushed cornflakes for breading to have extra crispiness.
Nutritional Information Per Serving:
Calories 266 | Fat 6.3g | Sodium 193mg | Carbs 39.1g | Fiber 7.2g | Sugar 5.2g | Protein 14.8g

Crusted Cod

Prep Time: 15 minutes.
Cook Time: 13 minutes.
Serves: 4

Ingredients:
- 2 lbs. cod fillets
- Salt, to taste
- Freshly black pepper, to taste
- ½ cup all-purpose flour
- 1 large egg, beaten
- 2 cups panko bread crumbs
- 1 teaspoon Old Bay seasoning
- Lemon wedges, for serving
- Tartar sauce, for serving

Preparation:
1. At 390 degrees F, preheat your Air Fryer on Air Fry mode.
2. Rub the fish with salt and black pepper.
3. Add flour in one shallow bowl, beat eggs in another bowl, and mix panko with Old Bay in a shallow bowl.
4. First, coat the fish with flour, then dip it in the eggs and finally coat it with the panko mixture.
5. Place the seasoned codfish in the Air Fryer Basket.
6. Return the Air Fryer Basket to the Air Fryer and cook for 13 minutes.
7. Initiate cooking by pressing the START/PAUSE BUTTON.
8. Flip the fish once cooked halfway, then resume cooking.
9. Serve warm and fresh with tartar sauce and lemon wedges.

Serving Suggestion: Enjoy with creamy coleslaw on the side.
Variation Tip: Use crushed cornflakes for extra crispiness.
Nutritional Information Per Serving:
Calories 155 | Fat 4.2g | Sodium 963mg | Carbs 21.5g | Fiber 0.8g | Sugar 5.7g | Protein 8.1g

Crusted Shrimp

Prep Time: 20 minutes.
Cook Time: 13 minutes.
Serves: 4
Ingredients:
- 1 lb. shrimp
- ½ cup flour, all-purpose
- 1 teaspoon salt
- ½ teaspoon baking powder
- ⅔ cup water
- 2 cups coconut shred
- ½ cup bread crumbs

Preparation:
1. At 390 degrees F, preheat your Air Fryer on Air Fry mode.
2. In a small bowl, whisk together flour, salt, water, and baking powder. Set aside for 5 minutes.
3. In another shallow bowl, toss bread crumbs with coconut shreds together.
4. Dredge shrimp in liquid, then coat in coconut mixture, making sure it's totally covered.
5. Repeat until all shrimp are coated.
6. Spread the shrimp in the Air Fryer Basket and spray them with cooking oil.
7. Return the Air Fryer Basket to the Air Fryer and cook for 13 minutes.
8. Initiate cooking by pressing the START/PAUSE BUTTON.
9. Shake the basket once cooked halfway, then resume cooking.
10. Serve with your favorite dip.

Serving Suggestion: Serve on top of mashed potato or mashed cauliflower.
Variation Tip: Use crushed cornflakes for breading to have extra crispiness.
Nutritional Information Per Serving:
Calories 297 | Fat 1g |Sodium 291mg | Carbs 35g | Fiber 1g | Sugar 9g | Protein 29g

Crispy Catfish

Prep Time: 15 minutes.
Cook Time: 17 minutes.
Serves: 4
Ingredients:
- 4 catfish fillets
- ¼ cup Louisiana Fish fry
- 1 tablespoon olive oil
- 1 tablespoon parsley, chopped
- 1 lemon, sliced
- Fresh herbs to garnish

Preparation:
1. At 390 degrees F, preheat your Air Fryer on Air Fry mode.
2. Mix fish fry with olive oil, and parsley then liberally rub over the catfish.
3. Place two fillets in the Air Fryer Basket.
4. Return the Air Fryer Basket to the Air Fryer and cook for 17 minutes.
5. Initiate cooking by pressing the START/PAUSE BUTTON.
6. Garnish with lemon slices and herbs.
7. Serve warm.

Serving Suggestion: Serve with creamy dip and crispy fries.
Variation Tip: Use crushed cornflakes for breading to have extra crispiness.
Nutritional Information Per Serving:
Calories 275 | Fat 1.4g |Sodium 582mg | Carbs 31.5g | Fiber 1.1g | Sugar 0.1g | Protein 29.8g

Savory Salmon Fillets

Prep Time: 10 minutes.
Cook Time: 17 minutes.
Serves: 4
Ingredients:
- 4 (6-oz) salmon fillets
- Salt, to taste
- Black pepper, to taste
- 4 teaspoons olive oil
- 4 tablespoons wholegrain mustard
- 2 tablespoons packed brown sugar
- 2 garlic cloves, minced
- 1 teaspoon thyme leaves

Preparation:
1. At 390 degrees F, preheat your Air Fryer on Air Fry mode.
2. Rub the salmon with salt and black pepper first.
3. Whisk oil with sugar, thyme, garlic, and mustard in a small bowl.
4. Place salmon fillets in the Air Fryer Basket and brush the thyme mixture on top of each fillet.
5. Return the Air Fryer Basket to the Air Fryer and cook for 17 minutes.
6. Initiate cooking by pressing the START/PAUSE BUTTON.
7. Serve warm and fresh.

Serving Suggestion: Serve with parsley and melted butter on top.
Variation Tip: Rub the fish fillets with lemon juice before cooking.
Nutritional Information Per Serving:
Calories 336 | Fat 6g | Sodium 181mg | Carbs 1.3g | Fiber 0.2g | Sugar 0.4g | Protein 69.2g

Fried Lobster Tails

Prep Time: 10 minutes.
Cook Time: 18 minutes.
Serves: 4
Ingredients:
- 4 (4 oz) lobster tails
- 8 tablespoons butter, melted
- 2 teaspoons lemon zest
- 2 garlic cloves, grated
- Salt and black pepper ground to taste
- 2 teaspoons fresh parsley, chopped
- 4 wedges lemon

Preparation:
1. At 350 degrees F, preheat your Air Fryer on Air Fry mode.
2. Spread the lobster tails into butterfly, slit the top to expose the lobster meat while keeping the tail intact.
3. Place the lobster tails in the Air Fryer Basket with their lobster meat facing up.
4. Mix melted butter with lemon zest and garlic in a bowl.
5. Brush the butter mixture on top of the lobster tails.
6. And drizzle salt and black pepper on top.
7. Return the Air Fryer Basket to the Air Fryer and cook for 18 minutes.
8. Initiate cooking by pressing the START/PAUSE BUTTON.
9. Garnish with parsley and lemon wedges.
10. Serve warm.

Serving Suggestion: Serve on a bed of lettuce leaves.
Variation Tip: Drizzle crushed cornflakes on top to have extra crispiness.
Nutritional Information Per Serving:
Calories 257 | Fat 10.4g | Sodium 431mg | Carbs 20g | Fiber 0g | Sugar 1.6g | Protein 21g

Buttered Mahi-Mahi

Prep Time: 15 minutes.
Cook Time: 22 minutes.
Serves: 4

Ingredients:
- 4 (6 oz) mahi-mahi fillets
- Salt and black pepper ground to taste
- Cooking spray
- ⅔ cup butter

Preparation:
1. At 390 degrees F, preheat your Air Fryer on Air Fry mode.
2. Rub the Mahi-mahi fillets with salt and black pepper.
3. Place mahi-mahi fillets in the Air Fryer's Basket.
4. Return the Air Fryer Basket to the Air Fryer and cook for 17 minutes.
5. Initiate cooking by pressing the START/PAUSE BUTTON.
6. Add butter to a saucepan and cook for 5 minutes until slightly brown.
7. Remove the butter from the heat.
8. Drizzle butter over the fish and serve warm.

Serving Suggestion: Serve with pasta or fried rice.

Variation Tip: Drizzle parmesan cheese on top.

Nutritional Information Per Serving:
Calories 399 | Fat 16g | Sodium 537mg | Carbs 28g | Fiber 3g | Sugar 10g | Protein 35g

Chapter 7-Vegetables Recipes

Stuffed Tomatoes

Prep Time: 12 Minutes
Cook Time: 8 Minutes
Serves: 2

Ingredients
- 2 cups brown rice, cooked
- 1 cup tofu, grilled and chopped
- 4 large red tomatoes
- 4 tablespoons basil, chopped
- ¼ tablespoon olive oil
- Salt and black pepper, to taste
- 2 tablespoons lemon juice
- 1 teaspoon red chili powder
- ½ cup Parmesan cheese

Directions
1. Take a large bowl and mix rice, tofu, basil, olive oil, salt, black pepper, lemon juice, and chili powder.
2. Take four large tomatoes and center core them.
3. Fill the cavity with the rice mixture.
4. Top it off with the cheese sprinkle.
5. Put the tomatoes into the air fryer basket.
6. Set it to AIR FRY mode, for 8 minutes at 400 degrees F.
7. Once done, serve and enjoy.

Serving Suggestion: Serve it with Greek yogurt.

Variation Tip: Use canola oil instead of olive oil.

Nutritional Information Per Serving: Calories 1034| Fat 24.2g| Sodium 527mg | Carbs 165g | Fiber 12.1g | Sugar 1.2g | Protein 43.9g

Saucy Carrots

Prep Time: 15 minutes.
Cook Time: 25 minutes.
Serves: 6

Ingredients:
- 1 lb. cup carrots, cut into chunks
- 1 tablespoon sesame oil
- ½ tablespoon ginger, minced
- ½ tablespoon soy sauce
- ½ teaspoon garlic, minced
- ½ tablespoon scallions, chopped, for garnish
- ½ teaspoon sesame seeds for garnish

Preparation:
1. At 390 degrees F, preheat your Air Fryer on Air Fry mode.
2. Toss all the ginger carrots ingredients, except the sesame seeds and scallions, in a suitable bowl.
3. Place the carrots in the Air Fryer Basket in a single layer.
4. Return the Air Fryer Basket to the Air Fryer and cook for 25 minutes.
5. Initiate cooking by pressing the START/PAUSE BUTTON.
6. Toss the carrots once cooked halfway through.
7. Garnish with sesame seeds and scallions.
8. Serve warm

Serving Suggestion: Serve with mayo sauce or ketchup.

Variation Tip: Use some honey for a sweet taste.

Nutritional Information Per Serving:
Calories 206 | Fat 3.4g |Sodium 174mg | Carbs 35g | Fiber 9.4g | Sugar 5.9g | Protein 10.6g

Zucchini with Stuffing

Prep Time: 12 Minutes
Cook Time: 20 Minutes
Serves: 3

Ingredients
- 1 cup quinoa, rinsed
- 1 cup black olives
- 6 medium zucchinis, about 2 pounds
- 2 cups cannellini beans, drained
- 1 white onion, chopped
- ¼ cup almonds, chopped
- 4 cloves garlic, chopped
- 4 tablespoons olive oil
- 1 cup water
- 2 cups Parmesan cheese, for topping

Directions
1. First wash the zucchini and cut it lengthwise.
2. Take a skillet and heat oil in it.
3. Sauté the onion in olive oil for a few minutes.
4. Then add the quinoa and water and let it cook for 8 minutes with the lid on the top.
5. Transfer the quinoa to a bowl and add all remaining ingredients excluding zucchini and Parmesan cheese.
6. Scoop out the seeds of zucchinis.
7. Fill the cavity of zucchinis with bowl mixture.
8. Top it with a handful of Parmesan cheese.
9. Arrange 4 zucchinis in the air fryer basket.
10. Select the AIR FRY for 20 minutes and adjust the temperature to 390 degrees F.
11. Once done, serve and enjoy.

Serving Suggestion: Serve it with pasta.
Variation Tip: None.
Nutritional Information Per Serving: Calories 1171| Fat 48.6g| Sodium 1747mg | Carbs 132.4g | Fiber 42.1g | Sugar 11.5g | Protein 65.7g

Green Beans with Baked Potatoes

Prep Time: 15 Minutes
Cook Time: 45 Minutes
Serves: 2

Ingredients
- 2 cups green beans
- 2 large potatoes, cubed
- 3 tablespoons olive oil
- 1 teaspoon seasoned salt
- ½ teaspoon chili powder
- ⅙ teaspoon garlic powder
- ¼ teaspoon onion powder

Directions
1. Take a large bowl and pour olive oil into it.
2. Now add all the seasoning in the olive oil and whisk it well.
3. Toss the green bean in it, and then transfer it to the basket of the air fryer.
4. Now season the potatoes with the seasoning and add them to the basket as well.
5. Now set the unit to AIR FRY mode at 350 degrees F for 45 minutes.
6. After 18 minutes take out the asparagus and continue with cooking.
7. Once the cooking cycle is complete, take out and serve it by transferring it to the serving plates.

Serving Suggestion: Serve with rice.
Variation Tip: Use canola oil instead of olive oil.
Nutritional Information Per Serving: Calories473 | Fat21.6g | Sodium796 mg | Carbs 66.6g | Fiber12.9 g | Sugar6 g | Protein8.4 g

Cheesy Potatoes with Asparagus

Prep Time: 15 Minutes
Cook Time: 35 Minutes
Serves: 2

Ingredients
- 1-½ pounds of russet potato, wedges or cut in half
- 2 teaspoons mixed herbs
- 2 teaspoons chili flakes
- 2 cups asparagus
- 1 cup chopped onion
- 1 tablespoon Dijon mustard
- ¼ cup fresh cream
- 1 teaspoon olive oil
- 2 tablespoons butter
- ½ teaspoon salt and black pepper
- Water as required
- ½ cup Parmesan cheese

Directions
1. Take a bowl and add asparagus and sweet potato wedges to it.
2. Season it with salt, black pepper, and olive oil.
3. Now add the potato wedges to the air fryer basket along with the asparagus.
4. Set it to AIR FRY mode at 390 degrees F for 30 minutes.
5. Meanwhile, take a skillet and add butter and sauté onion in it for a few minutes.
6. Then add salt and Dijon mustard and chili flakes, Parmesan cheese, and fresh cream.
7. Once cooking time passes 12 minutes, take out asparagus and continue cooking cycle.
8. Once it's done, take out the potato wedges.
9. Drizzle the skillet ingredients over the potatoes and serve with asparagus.

Serving Suggestion: Serve with rice.
Variation Tip: Use olive oil instead of butter.
Nutritional Information Per Serving: Calories 251| Fat11g | Sodium 279mg | Carbs 31.1g | Fiber 5g | Sugar 4.1g | Protein 9g

Kale and Spinach Chips

Prep Time: 12 Minutes
Cook Time: 8 Minutes
Serves: 2

Ingredients
- 2 cups spinach, torn in pieces and stem removed
- 2 cups kale, torn in pieces, stems removed
- 1 tablespoon olive oil
- Sea salt, to taste
- ⅓ cup Parmesan cheese

Directions
1. Take a bowl and add spinach to it.
2. Take another bowl and add kale to it.
3. Now, season both of them with olive oil, and sea salt.
4. Add kale and spinach to the basket of air fryer.
5. Select the AIR FRY mode at 350 degrees F for 8 minutes.
6. Once done, take out the crispy chips and sprinkle Parmesan cheese on top.
7. Serve and Enjoy.

Serving Suggestion: Serve it with baked potato.
Variation Tip: Use canola oil instead of olive oil.
Nutritional Information Per Serving: Calories 166| Fat 11.1g| Sodium 355mg | Carbs 8.1g | Fiber 1.7g | Sugar 0.1g | Protein 8.2g

Mixed Air Fry Veggies

Prep Time: 15 Minutes
Cook Time: 25 Minutes
Serves: 4

Ingredients
- 2 cups carrots, cubed
- 2 cups potatoes, cubed
- 2 cups shallots, cubed
- 2 cups zucchini, diced
- 2 cups yellow squash, cubed
- Salt and black pepper, to taste
- 1 tablespoon Italian seasoning
- 2 tablespoons ranch seasoning
- 4 tablespoons olive oil

Directions
1. Take a large bowl and add all the veggies to it.
2. Season the veggies with salt, pepper, Italian seasoning, ranch seasoning, and olive oil.
3. Toss all the ingredients well.
4. Now put it to the basket of the air fryer.
5. Set the unit to AIR FRY mode at 360 degrees F for 25 minutes.
6. Once it is cooked and done, serve, and enjoy.

Serving Suggestion: Serve it with rice.
Variation Tip: None.
Nutritional Information Per Serving: Calories 275| Fat 15.3g| Sodium 129mg | Carbs 33g | Fiber 3.8g | Sugar 5g | Protein 4.4g

Garlic Herbed Baked Potatoes

Prep Time: 25 Minutes
Cook Time: 45 Minutes
Serves: 4

Ingredients
- 4 large baking potatoes
- Salt and black pepper, to taste
- 2 teaspoons avocado oil

Cheese ingredients
- 2 cups sour cream
- 1 teaspoon garlic clove, minced
- 1 teaspoon fresh dill
- 2 teaspoons chopped chives
- Salt and black pepper, to taste
- 2 teaspoons Worcestershire sauce

Directions
1. Pierce the skin of potatoes with a fork.
2. Season the potatoes with olive oil, salt, and black pepper.
3. Put the potatoes into the basket of the Ninja Air Fryer.
4. Now set it to AIR FRY mode at 350 degrees F, for 45 minutes.
5. Meanwhile, take a bowl and mix all the ingredient under cheese ingredients.
6. Once the cooking cycle complete, take out and make a slit in-between the potatoes.
7. Add cheese mixture in the cavity and serve it hot.

Serving Suggestion: Serve with gravy.
Variation Tip: None.
Nutritional Information Per Serving: Calories 382| Fat24.6 g| Sodium 107mg | Carbs 36.2g | Fiber 2.5g | Sugar2 g | Protein 7.3g

Garlic Potato Wedges in Air Fryer

Prep Time: 10 Minutes
Cook Time: 20 Minutes
Serves: 2

Ingredients
- 4 medium potatoes, peeled and cut into wedges
- 4 tablespoons butter
- 1 teaspoon chopped cilantro
- 1 cup plain flour
- 1 teaspoon garlic, minced
- Salt and black pepper, to taste

Directions
1. Soak the potatoes wedges in cold water for about 30 minutes.
2. Then drain and pat dry with a paper towel.
3. Boil water in a large pot and boil the wedges just for 3 minutes.
4. Then take it out on a paper towel.
5. Now in bowl mix garlic, melted butter, salt, pepper, cilantro and whisk it well.
6. Add the flour to a separate bowl and add salt and black pepper.
7. Then add water to the flour so it gets runny in texture.
8. Now, coat the potatoes with flour mixture and add it to a foil tin.
9. Put foil tin in the air fryer basket.
10. Now, set time using AIR FRY mode at 390 degrees F for 20 minutes.
11. Once done, serve and enjoy.

Serving Suggestion: Serve with ketchup.
Variation Tip: Use olive oil instead of butter.
Nutritional Information Per Serving: Calories 727| Fat 24.1g| Sodium 191mg | Carbs 115.1g | Fiber 12g | Sugar 5.1g | Protein 14 g

Fresh Mix Veggies in Air Fryer

Prep Time: 15Minutes
Cook Time: 12 Minutes
Serves: 4

Ingredients
- 1 cup cauliflower florets
- 1 cup carrots, peeled chopped
- 1 cup broccoli florets
- 2 tablespoons avocado oil
- Salt, to taste
- ½ teaspoon chili powder
- ½ teaspoon garlic powder
- ½ teaspoon herbs de Provence
- 1 cup parmesan cheese

Directions
1. Take a bowl, and add all the veggies to it.
2. Toss and then season the veggies with salt, chili powder, garlic powder, and herbs de Provence.
3. Toss it all well and then drizzle avocado oil.
4. Make sure the ingredients are coated well.
5. Now transfer the veggies to the basket of the air fryer.
6. Turn on the start button and set it to AIR FRY mode at 390 degrees for 10-12 minutes.
7. After 8 minutes of cooking, select the pause button and then take out the basket and sprinkle Parmesan cheese on top of the veggies.
8. Then let the cooking cycle complete for the next 3-4 minutes.
9. Once done, serve.

Serving Suggestion: Serve it with rice.
Variation Tip: Use canola oil or butter instead of avocado oil.
Nutritional Information Per Serving: Calories161 | Fat 9.3g| Sodium 434mg | Carbs 7.7g | Fiber 2.4g | Sugar 2.5g | Protein 13.9

Brussels Sprouts

Prep Time: 15 Minutes
Cook Time: 20 Minutes
Serves: 2

Ingredients
- 2 pounds Brussels sprouts
- 2 tablespoons avocado oil
- Salt and pepper, to taste
- 1 cup pine nuts, roasted

Directions
1. Trim the bottom of Brussels sprouts.
2. Take a bowl and combine the avocado oil, salt, and black pepper.
3. Toss the Brussels sprouts well.
4. Transfer it to the air fryer basket.
5. Use AIR FRY mode for 20 minutes at 390 degrees F.
6. Once the Brussels sprouts get crisp and tender, take out and serve.

Serving Suggestion: Serve with rice.
Variation Tip: Use olive oil instead of avocado oil.
Nutritional Information Per Serving: Calories 672| Fat 50g| Sodium 115mg | Carbs 51g | Fiber 20.2g | Sugar 12.3g | Protein 25g

Curly Fries

Prep Time: 10 minutes.
Cook Time: 20 minutes.
Serves: 6

Ingredients:
- 2 spiralized zucchinis
- 1 cup flour
- 2 tablespoons paprika
- 1 teaspoon cayenne pepper
- 1 teaspoon garlic powder
- 1 teaspoon black pepper
- 1 teaspoon salt
- 2 eggs
- olive oil or cooking spray

Preparation:
1. At 390 degrees F, preheat your Air Fryer on Air Fry mode.
2. Mix flour with paprika, cayenne pepper, garlic powder, black pepper, and salt in a bowl.
3. Beat eggs in another bowl and dip the zucchini in the eggs.
4. Coat the zucchini with the flour mixture and place into the Air Fryer Basket.
5. Spray the zucchini with cooking oil.
6. Return the Air Fryer Basket to the Air Fryer and cook for 20 minutes.
7. Initiate cooking by pressing the START/PAUSE BUTTON.
8. Toss the zucchini once cooked halfway through, then resume cooking.
9. Serve warm.

Serving Suggestion: Serve with red chunky salsa or chili sauce.
Variation Tip: Use crushed cornflakes for breading to have extra crispiness.
Nutritional Information Per Serving:
Calories 212 | Fat 11.8g |Sodium 321mg | Carbs 24.6g | Fiber 4.4g | Sugar 8g | Protein 7.3g

Falafel

Prep Time: 15 minutes.
Cook Time: 14 minutes.
Serves: 6

Ingredients:
- 1 (15.5-oz) can chickpeas, rinsed and drained
- 1 small yellow onion, cut into quarters
- 3 garlic cloves, chopped
- ⅓ cup parsley, chopped
- ⅓ cup cilantro, chopped
- ⅓ cup scallions, chopped
- 1 teaspoon cumin
- ½ teaspoons salt
- ⅛ teaspoon crushed red pepper flakes
- 1 teaspoon baking powder
- 4 tablespoons all-purpose flour
- Olive oil spray

Preparation:
1. At 350 degrees F, preheat your Air Fryer on Air Fry mode.
2. Dry the chickpeas on paper towels.
3. Add onions and garlic to a food processor and chop them.
4. Add the parsley, salt, cilantro, scallions, cumin, and red pepper flakes.
5. Press the pulse button for 60 seconds, then toss in chickpeas and blend for 3 times until it makes a chunky paste.
6. Stir in baking powder and flour and mix well.
7. Transfer the falafel mixture to a bowl and cover to refrigerate for 3 hours.
8. Make 12 balls out of the falafel mixture.
9. Place falafels in the Air Fryer Basket and spray them with oil.
10. Return the Air Fryer Basket to the Air Fryer and cook for 14 minutes.
11. Initiate cooking by pressing the START/PAUSE BUTTON.
12. Toss the falafel once cooked halfway through, and resume cooking.
13. Serve warm.

Serving Suggestion: Serve with yogurt dip and sautéed carrots.
Variation Tip: Use breadcrumbs for breading to have extra crispiness.
Nutritional Information Per Serving:
Calories 113 | Fat 3g | Sodium 152mg | Carbs 20g | Fiber 3g | Sugar 1.1g | Protein 3.5g

Fried Artichoke Hearts

Prep Time: 15 minutes.
Cook Time: 10 minutes.
Serves: 6

Ingredients:
- 3 cans Quartered Artichokes, drained
- ½ cup mayonnaise
- 1 cup panko breadcrumbs
- ⅓ cup grated Parmesan
- salt and black pepper to taste
- Parsley for garnish

Preparation:
1. At 375 degrees F, preheat your Air Fryer on Air Fry mode.
2. Mix mayonnaise with salt and black pepper and keep the sauce aside.
3. Spread panko breadcrumbs in a bowl.
4. Coat the artichoke pieces with the breadcrumbs.
5. As you coat the artichokes, place them in the Air Fryer Basket in a single layer, then spray them with cooking oil.
6. Return the Air Fryer Basket to the Air Fryer and cook for 10 minutes.
7. Initiate cooking by pressing the START/PAUSE BUTTON.
8. Flip the artichokes once cooked halfway through, then resume cooking.
9. Serve warm with mayo sauce.

Serving Suggestion: Serve with red chunky salsa or chili sauce.
Variation Tip: Use crushed cornflakes for breading to have extra crispiness.
Nutritional Information Per Serving:
Calories 193 | Fat 1g | Sodium 395mg | Carbs 38.7g | Fiber 1.6g | Sugar 0.9g | Protein 6.6g

Lime Glazed Tofu

Prep Time: 10 minutes.
Cook Time: 14 minutes.
Serves: 6
Ingredients:
- ⅔ cup coconut aminos
- 2 (14-oz) packages extra-firm, water-packed tofu, drained
- 6 tablespoons toasted sesame oil
- ⅔ cup lime juice

Preparation:
1. At 400 degrees F, preheat your Air Fryer on Air Fry mode.
2. Pat dry the tofu bars and slice into half-inch cubes.
3. Toss all the remaining ingredients in a small bowl.
4. Marinate for 4 hours in the refrigerator. Drain off the excess water.
5. Place the tofu cubes in the Air Fryer Basket.
6. Return the Air Fryer Basket to the Air Fryer and cook for 14 minutes.
7. Initiate cooking by pressing the START/PAUSE BUTTON.
8. Toss the tofu once cooked halfway through, then resume cooking.
9. Serve warm.

Serving Suggestion: Serve with sautéed green vegetables.
Variation Tip: Add sautéed onion and carrot to the tofu cubes.
Nutritional Information Per Serving:
Calories 284 | Fat 7.9g | Sodium 704mg | Carbs 38.1g | Fiber 1.9g | Sugar 1.9g | Protein 14.8g

Sweet Potatoes with Honey Butter

Prep Time: 15 minutes.
Cook Time: 40 minutes.
Serves: 4
Ingredients:
- 4 sweet potatoes, scrubbed
- 1 teaspoon oil

Honey Butter
- 4 tablespoons unsalted butter
- 1 tablespoon honey
- 2 teaspoons hot sauce
- ¼ teaspoon salt

Preparation:
1. At 390 degrees F, preheat your Air Fryer on Air Fry mode.
2. Rub the sweet potatoes with oil and place two potatoes in the Air Fryer Basket.
3. Return the Air Fryer Basket to the Air Fryer and cook for 40 minutes.
4. Initiate cooking by pressing the START/PAUSE BUTTON.
5. Flip the potatoes once cooked halfway through, then resume cooking.
6. Mix butter with hot sauce, honey, and salt in a bowl.
7. When the potatoes are done, cut a slit on top and make a well with a spoon.
8. Pour the honey butter into each potato jacket.
9. Serve.

Serving Suggestion: Serve with sautéed vegetables and salad.
Variation Tip: Sprinkle crumbled bacon and parsley on top.
Nutritional Information Per Serving:
Calories 288 | Fat 6.9g | Sodium 761mg | Carbs 46g | Fiber 4g | Sugar 12g | Protein 9.6g

Zucchini Cakes

Prep Time: 10 minutes.
Cook Time: 32 minutes.
Serves: 6
Ingredients:
- 2 medium zucchinis, grated
- 1 cup corn kernel
- 1 medium potato cooked
- 2 tablespoons chickpea flour
- 2 garlic minced
- 2 teaspoons olive oil
- Salt and black pepper

For Serving:
- Yogurt tahini sauce

Preparation:
1. At 390 degrees F, preheat your Air Fryer on Air Fry mode.
2. Mix grated zucchini with a pinch of salt in a colander and leave them for 15 minutes.
3. Squeeze out their excess water.
4. Mash the cooked potato in a large-sized bowl with a fork.
5. Add zucchini, corn, garlic, chickpea flour, salt, and black pepper to the bowl.
6. Mix these fritters' ingredients together and make 2 tablespoons-sized balls out of this mixture and flatten them lightly.
7. Place the fritters in the Air Fryer Basket in a single layer and spray them with cooking.
8. Return the Air Fryer Basket to the Air Fryer and cook for 17 minutes.
9. Initiate cooking by pressing the START/PAUSE BUTTON.
10. Flip the fritters once cooked halfway through, then resume cooking.
11. Serve.

Serving Suggestion: Serve with mayonnaise or cream cheese dip.
Variation Tip: Use crushed cornflakes for breading to have extra crispiness.
Nutritional Information Per Serving:
Calories 270 | Fat 14.6g |Sodium 394mg | Carbs 31.3g | Fiber 7.5g | Sugar 9.7g | Protein 6.4g

Hasselback Potatoes

Prep Time: 15 minutes.
Cook Time: 15 minutes.
Serves: 4
Ingredients:
- 4 medium Yukon Gold potatoes
- 3 tablespoons melted butter
- 1 tablespoon olive oil
- 3 garlic cloves, crushed
- ½ teaspoon ground paprika
- Salt and black pepper ground, to taste
- 1 tablespoon chopped fresh parsley

Preparation:
1. At 375 degrees F, preheat your Air Fryer on Air Fry mode.
2. Slice each potato from the top to make ¼-inch slices without cutting its ½-inch bottom, keeping the potato's bottom intact.
3. Mix butter with olive oil, garlic, and paprika in a small bowl.
4. Brush the garlic mixture on top of each potato and add the mixture into the slits.
5. Season them with salt and black pepper.
6. Place the seasoned potatoes in the Air Fryer Basket
7. Return the Air Fryer Basket to the Air Fryer and cook for 25 minutes.
8. Initiate cooking by pressing the START/PAUSE BUTTON.
9. Brushing the potatoes again with butter mixture after 15 minutes, then resume cooking.
10. Garnish with parsley.
11. Serve warm.

Serving Suggestion: Serve with mayonnaise or cream cheese dip.
Variation Tip: Add tomato and cheese slices to the potato slits before air frying.
Nutritional Information Per Serving:
Calories 350 | Fat 2.6g |Sodium 358mg | Carbs 64.6g | Fiber 14.4g | Sugar 3.3g | Protein 19.9g

Air Fried Okra

Prep Time: 10 minutes.
Cook Time: 13 minutes.
Serves: 2
Ingredients:
- ½ lb. okra pods sliced
- 1 teaspoon olive oil
- ¼ teaspoon salt
- ⅛ teaspoon black pepper

Preparation:
1. At 375 degrees F, preheat your Air Fryer on Air Fry mode.
2. Toss okra with olive oil, salt, and black pepper in a bowl.
3. Spread the okra in a single layer in the Air Fryer Basket.
4. Return the Air Fryer Basket to the Air Fryer and cook for 13 minutes.
5. Initiate cooking by pressing the START/PAUSE BUTTON.
6. Toss the okra once cooked halfway through, and resume cooking.
7. Serve warm.

Serving Suggestion: Serve with potato chips and bread slices.
Variation Tip: Sprinkle cornmeal before cooking for added crispiness.
Nutritional Information Per Serving:
Calories 208 | Fat 5g | Sodium 1205mg | Carbs 34.1g | Fiber 7.8g | Sugar 2.5g | Protein 5.9g

Fried Olives

Prep Time: 15 minutes.
Cook Time: 9 minutes.
Serves: 6
Ingredients:
- 2 cups blue cheese stuffed olives, drained
- ½ cup all-purpose flour
- 1 cup panko breadcrumbs
- ½ teaspoon garlic powder
- 1 pinch oregano
- 2 eggs

Preparation:
1. At 375 degrees F, preheat your Air Fryer on Air Fry mode.
2. Mix flour with oregano and garlic powder in a bowl and beat two eggs in another bowl.
3. Spread panko breadcrumbs in a bowl.
4. Coat all the olives with the flour mixture, dip in the eggs and then coat with the panko breadcrumbs.
5. As you coat the olives, place them in the Air Fryer Basket in a single layer, then spray them with cooking oil.
6. Return the Air Fryer Basket to the Air Fryer and cook for 9 minutes.
7. Initiate cooking by pressing the START/PAUSE BUTTON.
8. Flip the olives once cooked halfway through, then resume cooking.
9. Serve.

Serving Suggestion: Serve with red chunky salsa or chili sauce.
Variation Tip: Use crushed cornflakes for breading to have extra crispiness.
Nutritional Information Per Serving:
Calories 166 | Fat 3.2g | Sodium 437mg | Carbs 28.8g | Fiber 1.8g | Sugar 2.7g | Protein 5.8g

Quinoa Patties

Prep Time: 15 minutes.
Cook Time: 32 minutes.
Serves: 4

Ingredients:
- 1 cup quinoa red
- 1½ cups water
- 1 teaspoon salt
- black pepper, ground
- 1½ cups rolled oats
- 3 eggs beaten
- ¼ cup minced white onion
- ½ cup crumbled feta cheese
- ¼ cup chopped fresh chives
- Salt and black pepper, to taste
- Vegetable or canola oil
- 4 hamburger buns
- 4 arugulas
- 4 slices tomato sliced

Cucumber yogurt dill sauce
- 1 cup cucumber, diced
- 1 cup Greek yogurt
- 2 teaspoons lemon juice
- ¼ teaspoon salt
- Black pepper, ground
- 1 tablespoon chopped fresh dill
- 1 tablespoon olive oil

Preparation:
1. At 390 degrees F, preheat your Air Fryer on Air Fry mode.
2. Add quinoa to a saucepan filled with cold water, salt, and black pepper, and place it over medium-high heat.
3. Cook the quinoa to a boil, then reduce the heat, cover, and cook for 20 minutes on a simmer.
4. Fluff and mix the cooked quinoa with a fork and remove it from the heat.
5. Spread the quinoa in a baking stay.
6. Mix eggs, oats, onion, herbs, cheese, salt, and black pepper.
7. Stir in quinoa, then mix well. Make 4 patties out of this quinoa cheese mixture.
8. Place the patties in the Air Fryer Basket and spray them with cooking oil.
9. Return the Air Fryer Basket to the Air Fryer and cook for 13 minutes.
10. Initiate cooking by pressing the START/PAUSE BUTTON.
11. Flip the patties once cooked halfway through, and resume cooking.
12. Meanwhile, prepare the cucumber yogurt dill sauce by mixing all of its ingredients in a mixing bowl.
13. Place each quinoa patty in a burger bun along with arugula leaves.
14. Serve with yogurt dill sauce.

Serving Suggestion: Serve with yogurt dip.
Variation Tip: Use crushed cornflakes for breading to have extra crispiness.
Nutritional Information Per Serving:
Calories 231 | Fat 9g |Sodium 271mg | Carbs 32.8g | Fiber 6.4g | Sugar 7g | Protein 6.3g

Chapter 8-Desserts Recipes

Cake in the Air Fryer

Prep Time: 12 Minutes
Cook Time: 30 Minutes
Serves: 2
Ingredients
- 90 grams all-purpose flour
- 1 Pinch of salt
- ½ teaspoon baking powder
- ½ cup tutti-fruitti mix
- 2 eggs
- 1 teaspoon vanilla extract
- 10 tablespoons white sugar

Directions
1. Take a bowl and add all-purpose flour, salt, and baking powder.
2. Stir it in a large bowl.
3. Whisk two eggs in a separate bowl and add vanilla extract, sugar and blend it with a hand beater.
4. Now combine wet ingredients with the dry ones.
5. Mix it well and pour it into round pan that fits inside basket.
6. Place the pan inside the basket.
7. Now set it to Air Fry function at 310 degrees F for 30 minutes.
8. Once it's done, serve and enjoy.

Serving Suggestion: Serve it with whipped cream.
Variation Tip: Use brown sugar instead of white sugar.
Nutritional Information Per Serving: Calories 711| Fat4.8g| Sodium 143mg | Carbs 161g | Fiber 1.3g | Sugar 105g | Protein 10.2g

Bread Pudding

Prep Time: 12 Minutes
Cook Time: 8-12 Minutes
Serves: 2
Ingredients
- Nonstick spray, for greasing ramekins
- 2 slices white bread, crumbled
- 4 tablespoons white sugar
- 5 large eggs
- ½ cup cream
- Salt, pinch
- ⅓ teaspoon cinnamon powder

Directions
1. Take a bowl and whisk eggs in it.
2. Add sugar and salt to the egg and whisk it all well.
3. Then add cream and use a hand beater to incorporate the entire ingredients.
4. Now add cinnamon, and add crumbs of bread.
5. Mix it well and add into a round shaped baking pan.
6. Put it inside the Ninja Air Fryer.
7. Set it on AIR FRY mode at 350 degrees F for 8-12 minutes.
8. Once it's cooked, serve.

Serving Suggestion: Serve it with Coffee.
Variation Tip: Use brown sugar instead of white sugar.
Nutritional Information Per Serving: Calories 331| Fat16.1g| Sodium 331mg | Carbs 31g | Fiber0.2g | Sugar 26.2g | Protein 16.2g

Tasty Pumpkin Muffins

Prep Time: 20 Minutes
Cook Time: 19 Minutes
Serves: 4

Ingredients
- 1 and ½ cups all-purpose flour
- ½ teaspoon baking soda
- ½ teaspoon of baking powder
- 1 and ¼ teaspoons cinnamon, groaned
- ¼ teaspoon ground nutmeg, grated
- 2 large eggs
- Salt, pinch
- ¾ cup granulated sugar
- ½ cup dark brown sugar
- 1 and ½ cups of pumpkin puree
- ¼ cup coconut milk

Directions
1. Take 4 ramekins that are the size of a cup and layer them with muffin papers.
2. Crack an egg in a bowl and add brown sugar, baking soda, baking powder, cinnamon, nutmeg, and sugar.
3. Whisk it all very well with an electric hand beater.
4. Now, in a second bowl, mix the flour, and salt.
5. Now, mix the dry ingredients slowly with the wet ingredients.
6. Now, at the end fold in the pumpkin puree and milk, mix it well
7. Divide this batter into 4 ramekins.
8. Now, put the ramekins inside the basket.
9. Add basket to the unit.
10. Set the time to 18 minutes at 360 degrees F at AIR FRY mode.
11. Check if not done, and let it AIR FRY for one more minute.
12. Once it is done, serve.

Serving Suggestion: Serve it with a glass of milk.
Variation Tip: Use almond milk instead of coconut milk.
Nutritional Information Per Serving: Calories 291| Fat6.4 g| Sodium 241mg | Carbs 57.1g | Fiber 4.4g | Sugar42 g | Protein 5.9g

Air Fryer Sweet Twists

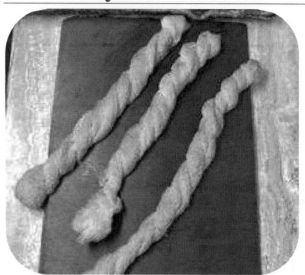

Prep Time: 15 Minutes
Cook Time: 10 Minutes
Serves: 2

Ingredients
- 1 box store-bought puff pastry
- ½ teaspoon cinnamon
- ½ teaspoon sugar
- ½ teaspoon black sesame seeds
- Salt, pinch
- 2 tablespoons Parmesan cheese, freshly grated

Directions
1. Place the dough on a work surface.
2. Take a small bowl and mix cheese, sugar, salt, sesame seeds, and cinnamon.
3. Press this mixture on both sides of the dough.
4. Now, cut the pastry into 1" x 3" strips.
5. Twist each of the strips 2 times and then lay it onto the flat.
6. Transfer it to the air fryer basket.
7. Select the AIR FRY mode at 400 degrees F for 10 minutes.
8. Once cooked, serve.

Serving Suggestion: Serve it with champagne!
Variation Tip: None.
Nutritional Information Per Serving: Calories 140| Fat9.4g| Sodium 142mg | Carbs 12.3g | Fiber0.8 g | Sugar 1.2g | Protein 2g

Mini Strawberry and Cream Pies

Prep Time: 12 Minutes
Cook Time: 10 Minutes
Serves: 2

Ingredients
- 1 box Store-Bought Pie Dough, Trader Joe's
- 1 cup strawberries, cubed
- 3 tablespoons cream, heavy
- 2 tablespoons almonds
- 1 egg white, for brushing

Directions
1. Take the store brought pie dough and flatten it on a surface.
2. Use a round cutter to cut it into 3-inch circles.
3. Brush the dough with egg white all around the parameters.
4. Now add almonds, strawberries, and cream in a very little amount in the center of the dough, and top it with another circular.
5. Press the edges with the fork to seal it.
6. Make a slit in the middle of the dough and put it into the basket.
7. Set it to AIR FRY mode 360 degrees for 10 minutes.
8. Once done, serve.

Serving Suggestion: Serve it with vanilla ice-cream.
Variation Tip: Use orange zest instead of lemon zest.
Nutritional Information Per Serving: Calories 203| Fat12.7g| Sodium 193mg | Carbs20 g | Fiber 2.2g | Sugar 5.8g | Protein 3.7g

Lemony Sweet Twists

Prep Time: 15 Minutes
Cook Time: 9 Minutes
Serves: 2

Ingredients
- 1 box store-bought puff pastry
- ½ teaspoon lemon zest
- 1 tablespoon lemon juice
- 2 teaspoons brown sugar
- Salt, pinch
- 2 tablespoons Parmesan cheese, freshly grated

Directions
1. Put the puff pastry dough on a clean work area.
2. In a bowl, combine Parmesan cheese, brown sugar, salt, lemon zest, and lemon juice.
3. Press this mixture on both sides of the dough.
4. Now, cut the pastry into 1" x 4" strips.
5. Twist each of the strips.
6. Transfer it to the air fryer basket.
7. Select the air fry mode at 400 degrees F for 9-10 minutes.
8. Once cooked, serve and enjoy.

Serving Suggestion: Serve it with champagne!
Variation Tip: None.
Nutritional Information Per Serving: Calories 156| Fat10g| Sodium 215mg | Carbs 14g | Fiber 0.4g | Sugar3.3 g | Protein 2.8g

Chocolate Chip Muffins

Prep Time: 12 Minutes
Cook Time: 15 Minutes
Serves: 2
Ingredients
- Salt, pinch
- 2 eggs
- ⅓ cup brown sugar
- ⅓ cup butter
- 4 tablespoons milk
- ¼ teaspoon vanilla extract
- ½ teaspoon baking powder
- 1 cup all-purpose flour
- 1 pouch chocolate chips, 35 grams

Directions
1. Take 4 oven-safe ramekins that are the size of a cup and layer them with muffin papers.
2. In a bowl, whisk the egg, brown sugar, butter, milk, and vanilla extract.
3. Whisk it all very well with an electric hand beater.
4. Now, in a second bowl, mix the flour, baking powder, and salt.
5. Now, mix the dry ingredients slowly into the wet ingredients.
6. Now, at the end fold in the chocolate chips and mix them well.
7. Divide this batter into 4 ramekins.
8. Now, put the ramekins in the basket.
9. Set the time to 15 minutes at 350 degrees F, on AIR FRY mode.
10. Check if not done, and let it AIR FRY for one more minute.
11. Once it is done, serve.

Serving Suggestion: Serve it with chocolate syrup drizzle.
Variation Tip: None.
Nutritional Information Per Serving: Calories 757| Fat40.3g| Sodium 426mg | Carbs 85.4g | Fiber 2.2g | Sugar 30.4g | Protein 14.4g

Chocolate Chip Cake

Prep Time: 12 Minutes
Cook Time: 15 Minutes
Serves: 4servings
Ingredients
- Salt, pinch
- 2 eggs, whisked
- ½ cup brown sugar
- ½ cup butter, melted
- 10 tablespoons almond milk
- ¼ teaspoon vanilla extract
- ½ teaspoon baking powder
- 1 cup all-purpose flour
- 1 cup chocolate chips
- ½ cup cocoa powder

Directions
1. Take a large baking pan that fits inside the basket of the air fryer.
2. Layer it with baking paper, cut it to the size of a baking pan.
3. In a bowl, whisk the egg, brown sugar, butter, almond milk, and vanilla extract.
4. Whisk it all very well with an electric hand beater.
5. In a second bowl, mix the flour, cocoa powder, baking powder, and salt.

6. Now, mix the dry ingredients slowly with the wet ingredients.
7. Now, at the end fold in the chocolate chips.
8. Incorporate all the ingredients well.
9. Pour this batter into the round baking pan.
10. Put it inside the basket.
11. Set the time to 15 minutes at 350 degrees F at AIR FRY mode.
12. Check if not done, and let it AIR FRY for one more minute.
13. Once it is done, serve.

Serving Suggestion: Serve it with chocolate syrup drizzle.
Variation Tip: Use baking soda instead of baking powder.
Nutritional Information Per Serving: Calories 736| Fat 45.5g| Sodium 356mg | Carbs 78.2g | Fiber 6.1g | Sugar 32.7g | Protein 11.5 g

Mini Blueberry Pies

Prep Time: 12 Minutes
Cook Time: 10 Minutes
Serves: 2

Ingredients
- 1 box store-bought pie dough, Trader Joe's
- ¼ cup blueberry jam
- 1 teaspoon lemon zest
- 1 egg white, for brushing

Directions
1. Take the store brought pie dough and cut it into 3-inch circles.
2. Brush the dough with egg white all around the parameters.
3. Now add blueberry jam and zest in the middle and top it with another circular.
4. Press the edges with the fork to seal it.
5. Make a slit in the middle of the dough and transfer it to the basket.
6. Set it to AIR FRY mode at 360 degrees for 10 minutes.
7. Once cooked, serve.

Serving Suggestion: Serve it with vanilla ice-cream.
Variation Tip: Use orange zest instead of lemon zest.
Nutritional Information Per Serving: Calories 234| Fat 8.6g| Sodium 187mg | Carbs 38.2 g | Fiber 0.1g | Sugar 13.7 g | Protein 2g

Apple Hand Pies

Prep Time: 15 minutes.
Cook Time: 21 minutes.
Serves: 8

Ingredients:
- 8 tablespoons butter, softened
- 12 tablespoons brown sugar
- 2 teaspoons cinnamon, ground
- 4 medium Granny Smith apples, diced
- 2 teaspoons cornstarch
- 4 teaspoons cold water
- 1 (14 oz) package pastry, 9-inch crust pie
- Cooking spray
- 1 tablespoon grapeseed oil
- ½ cup powdered sugar
- 2 teaspoons milk

Preparation:
1. At 390 degrees F, preheat your Air Fryer on Air Fry mode.
2. Toss apples with brown sugar, butter, and cinnamon in a suitable skillet.
3. Place the skillet over medium heat and stir cook for 5 minutes.
4. Mix cornstarch with cold water in a small bowl.
5. Add cornstarch mixture into the apple and cook for 1 minute until it thickens.
6. Remove this filling from the heat and allow it to cool.

7. Unroll the pie crust and spray on a floured surface.
8. Cut the dough into 16 equal rectangles.
9. Wet the edges of the 8 rectangles with water and divide the apple filling at the center of these rectangles.
10. Place the other 8 rectangles on top and crimp the edges with a fork, then make 2-3 slashes on top.
11. Place the small pies in the Air Fryer Basket.
12. Return the Air Fryer Basket to the Air Fryer and cook for 17 minutes.
13. Initiate cooking by pressing the START/PAUSE BUTTON.
14. Flip the pies once cooked halfway through, and resume cooking.
15. Meanwhile, mix sugar with milk.
16. Pour this mixture over the apple pies.
17. Serve fresh.

Serving Suggestion: Serve with apple sauce.
Variation Tip: Add shredded nuts and coconuts to the filling.
Nutritional Information Per Serving:
Calories 284 | Fat 16g | Sodium 252mg | Carbs 31.6g | Fiber 0.9g | Sugar 6.6g | Protein 3.7g

Apple Nutmeg Flautas

Prep Time: 10 minutes.
Cook Time: 8 minutes.
Serves: 8
Ingredients:
- ¼ cup light brown sugar
- ⅛ cup all-purpose flour
- ¼ teaspoon ground cinnamon
- Nutmeg, to taste
- 4 apples, peeled, cored & sliced
- ½ lemon, juice, and zest
- 6 (10-inch) flour tortillas
- Vegetable oil
- Caramel sauce
- Cinnamon sugar

Preparation:
1. At 400 degrees F, preheat your Air Fryer on Air Fry mode.
2. Mix brown sugar with cinnamon, nutmeg, and flour in a large bowl.
3. Toss in apples in lemon juice. Mix well.
4. Place a tortilla at a time on a flat surface and add ½ cup of the apple mixture to the tortilla.
5. Roll the tortilla into a burrito and seal it tightly and hold it in place with a toothpick.
6. Repeat the same steps with the remaining tortillas and apple mixture.
7. Place the apple burritos in the Air Fryer Basket and spray them with cooking oil.
8. Return the Air Fryer Basket to the Air Fryer and cook for 8 minutes.
9. Initiate cooking by pressing the START/PAUSE BUTTON.
10. Flip the burritos once cooked halfway through, then resume cooking.
11. Garnish with caramel sauce and cinnamon sugar.
12. Enjoy.

Serving Suggestion: Serve with maple syrup on the side.
Variation Tip: Add orange juice and zest for change of taste.
Nutritional Information Per Serving:
Calories 157 | Fat 1.3g | Sodium 27mg | Carbs 1.3g | Fiber 1g | Sugar 2.2g | Protein 8.2g

Air Fried Beignets

Prep Time: 15 minutes.
Cook Time: 21 minutes.
Serves: 6
Ingredients:
- Cooking spray
- ¼ cup white sugar
- ⅛ cup water
- ½ cup all-purpose flour
- 1 large egg, separated
- 1 ½ teaspoons butter, melted

- ½ teaspoon baking powder
- ½ teaspoon vanilla extract
- 1 pinch salt
- 2 tablespoons confectioners' sugar, or to taste

Preparation:
1. At 390 degrees F, preheat your Air Fryer on Air Fry mode.
2. Beat flour with water, sugar, egg yolk, baking powder, butter, vanilla extract, and salt in a large bowl until lumps-free.
3. Beat egg whites in a separate bowl and beat using an electric hand mixer until it forms soft peaks.
4. Add the egg white to the flour batter and mix gently until fully incorporated.
5. Divide the dough into small beignets and place them in the Air Fryer Basket.
6. Return the Air Fryer Basket to the Air Fryer and cook for 17 minutes.
7. Initiate cooking by pressing the START/PAUSE BUTTON.
8. And cook for another 4 minutes. Dust the cooked beignets with sugar.
9. Serve.

Serving Suggestion: Serve with a dollop of sweet cream dip.
Variation Tip: Add chopped raisins and nuts to the dough.
Nutritional Information Per Serving:
Calories 327 | Fat 14.2g |Sodium 672mg | Carbs 47.2g | Fiber 1.7g | Sugar 24.8g | Protein 4.4g

Air Fried Bananas

Prep Time: 10 minutes.
Cook Time: 13 minutes.
Serves: 4
Ingredients:
- 4 bananas, sliced
- 1 avocado oil cooking spray

Preparation:
1. At 350 degrees F, preheat your Air Fryer on Air Fry mode.
2. Spread the banana slices in the Air Fryer Basket in a single layer.
3. Drizzle avocado oil over the banana slices.
4. Return the Air Fryer Basket to the Air Fryer and cook for 13 minutes.
5. Initiate cooking by pressing the START/PAUSE BUTTON.
6. Serve.

Serving Suggestion: Serve with a dollop of vanilla ice-cream.
Variation Tip: Drizzle chopped nuts on top of the bananas.
Nutritional Information Per Serving:
Calories 149 | Fat 1.2g |Sodium 3mg | Carbs 37.6g | Fiber 5.8g | Sugar 29g | Protein 1.1g

Apple Crisp

Prep Time: 15 minutes.
Cook Time: 14 minutes.
Serves: 8
Ingredients:
- 3 cups apples, chopped
- 1 tablespoon pure maple syrup
- 2 teaspoons lemon juice
- 3 tablespoons all-purpose flour
- ⅓ cup quick oats
- ¼ cup brown sugar
- 2 tablespoons light butter, melted
- ½ teaspoon cinnamon

Preparation:
1. At 375 degrees F, preheat your Air Fryer on Air Fry mode.
2. Toss the chopped apples with 1 tablespoon of all-purpose flour, cinnamon, maple syrup, and lemon juice in a suitable bowl.

3. Add the apples in the Air Fryer Basket with its crisper plate.
4. Whisk oats, brown sugar, and remaining all-purpose flour in a small bowl.
5. Stir in melted butter, then spread this mixture over the apples.
6. Return the Air Fryer Basket to the Air Fryer and cook for 14 minutes.
7. Initiate cooking by pressing the START/PAUSE BUTTON.
8. Enjoy fresh.
Serving Suggestion: Serve with a warming cup of hot chocolate.
Variation Tip: Use crushed cookies or graham crackers instead of oats.
Nutritional Information Per Serving:
Calories 258 | Fat 12.4g |Sodium 79mg | Carbs 34.3g | Fiber 1g | Sugar 17g | Protein 3.2g

Zesty Cranberry Scones

Prep Time: 10 minutes.
Cook Time: 16 minutes.
Serves: 8
Ingredients:
- 4 cups of flour
- ½ cup brown sugar
- 2 tablespoons baking powder
- ½ teaspoon ground nutmeg
- ½ teaspoon salt
- ½ cup butter, chilled and diced
- 2 cups fresh cranberry
- ⅔ cup sugar
- 2 tablespoons orange zest
- 1 ¼ cups half and half cream
- 2 eggs

Preparation:
1. At 375 degrees F, preheat your Air Fryer on Air Fry mode.
2. Whisk flour with baking powder, salt, nutmeg, and both the sugars in a bowl.
3. Stir in egg and cream, mix well to form a smooth dough.
4. Fold in cranberries along with the orange zest.
5. Knead this dough well on a work surface.
6. Cut 3-inch circles out of the dough.
7. Place the scones in the Air Fryer Basket and spray them with cooking oil.
8. Return the Air Fryer Basket to the Air Fryer and cook for 16 minutes.
9. Initiate cooking by pressing the START/PAUSE BUTTON.
10. Flip the scones once cooked halfway and resume cooking.
11. Enjoy.
Serving Suggestion: Serve with cranberry jam on the side.
Variation Tip: Add raisins instead of cranberries to the dough.
Nutritional Information Per Serving:
Calories 204 | Fat 9g |Sodium 91mg | Carbs 27g | Fiber 2.4g | Sugar 15g | Protein 1.3g

Walnuts Fritters

Prep Time: 15 minutes.
Cook Time: 15 minutes.
Serves: 6
Ingredients:
- 1 cup all-purpose flour
- ½ cup walnuts, chopped
- ¼ cup white sugar
- ¼ cup milk
- 1 egg
- 1½ teaspoons baking powder
- 1 pinch salt
- Cooking spray
- 2 tablespoons white sugar
- ½ teaspoon ground cinnamon

Glaze:
- ½ cup confectioners' sugar
- 1 tablespoon milk
- ½ teaspoon caramel extract
- ¼ teaspoon ground cinnamon

Preparation:
1. At 375 degrees F, preheat your Air Fryer on Air Fry mode.
2. Layer the Air Fryer Basket with parchment paper.

3. Grease the parchment paper with cooking spray.
4. Whisk flour with milk, ¼ cup of sugar, egg, baking powder, and salt in a small bowl.
5. Separately mix 2 tablespoons of sugar with cinnamon in another bowl, toss in walnuts and mix well to coat.
6. Stir in flour mixture and mix until combined.
7. Drop the fritters mixture using a cookie scoop into the Air Fryer Basket.
8. Return the Air Fryer Basket to the Air Fryer and cook for 15 minutes.
9. Initiate cooking by pressing the START/PAUSE BUTTON.
10. Flip the fritters once cooked halfway through, then resume cooking.
11. Meanwhile, whisk milk, caramel extract, confectioners' sugar, and cinnamon in a bowl.
12. Transfer fritters to a wire rack and allow them to cool.
13. Drizzle with a glaze over the fritters.

Serving Suggestion: Serve with butter pecan ice cream or strawberry jam.
Variation Tip: Add maple syrup on top.
Nutritional Information Per Serving:
Calories 391 | Fat 24g |Sodium 142mg | Carbs 38.5g | Fiber 3.5g | Sugar 21g | Protein 6.6g

Oreo Rolls

Prep Time: 10 minutes.
Cook Time: 12 minutes.
Serves: 9
Ingredients:
- 1 crescent sheet roll
- 9 Oreo cookies
- Cinnamon powder, to serve
- Powdered sugar, to serve

Preparation:

1. At 360 degrees F, preheat your Air Fryer on Air Fry mode.
2. Spread the crescent sheet roll and cut it into 9 equal squares.
3. Place one cookie at the center of each square.
4. Wrap each square around the cookies and press the ends to seal.
5. Place half of the wrapped cookies in the Air Fryer Basket.
6. Return the Air Fryer Basket to the Air Fryer and cook for 6 minutes.
7. Initiate cooking by pressing the START/PAUSE BUTTON.
8. Cook the remaining cookie rolls in the same way.
9. Garnish the rolls with sugar and cinnamon.
10. Serve.

Serving Suggestion: Serve a cup of spice latte or hot chocolate.
Variation Tip: Dip the rolls in melted chocolate for a change of taste.
Nutritional Information Per Serving:
Calories 175 | Fat 13.1g |Sodium 154mg | Carbs 14g | Fiber 0.8g | Sugar 8.9g | Protein 0.7g

Biscuit Doughnuts

Prep Time: 15 minutes.
Cook Time: 15 minutes.
Serves: 8
Ingredients:
- ½ cup white sugar
- 1 teaspoon cinnamon
- ½ cup powdered sugar
- 1 can pre-made biscuit dough
- Coconut oil
- Melted butter to brush biscuits

Preparation:

1. At 375 degrees F, preheat your Air Fryer on Air Fry mode.

2. Place all the biscuits on a cutting board and cut holes in the center of each biscuit using a cookie cutter.
3. Grease the Air Fryer Basket with coconut oil.
4. Place the biscuits in the Air Fryer Basket while keeping them 1 inch apart.
5. Return the Air Fryer Basket to the Air Fryer and cook for 15 minutes.
6. Initiate cooking by pressing the START/PAUSE BUTTON.
7. Brush all the donuts with melted butter and sprinkle cinnamon and sugar on top.
8. Air Fry these donuts for one minute more.
9. Enjoy.

Serving Suggestion: Serve the doughnuts with chocolate syrup on top.

Variation Tip: Inject strawberry jam into each doughnut.

Nutritional Information Per Serving:
Calories 192 | Fat 9.3g | Sodium 133mg | Carbs 27.1g | Fiber 1.4g | Sugar 19g | Protein 3.2g

Fudge Brownies

Prep Time: 20 Minutes
Cook Time: 35 Minutes
Serves: 4

Ingredients
- ½ cup all-purpose flour
- ¼ cup unsweetened cocoa powder
- ¾ teaspoon kosher salt
- 2 large eggs, whisked
- 1 tablespoon almond milk
- ½ cup brown sugar
- ½ cup packed white sugar
- ½ tablespoon vanilla extract
- 8 ounces of semisweet chocolate chips, melted
- ½ cup unsalted butter, melted

Directions
1. Take a medium bowl, and use a hand beater to whisk together eggs, milk, both the sugars and vanilla.
2. In a separate microwave-safe bowl, mix melted butter and chocolate and microwave it for 30 seconds to melt the chocolate.
3. Add all the listed dry ingredients to the chocolate mixture.
4. Now incorporate the egg bowl ingredient into the batter.
5. Spray a reasonable size round baking pan that fits in basket of air fryer.
6. Grease the pan with cooking spray.
7. Now pour the batter into the pan, put the crisper plate in basket.
8. Add the pan and insert the basket into the unit.
9. Select the AIR FRY mode and adjust the temperature to 300 degrees F and the time to 30 minutes.
10. Check it after 35 minutes and if not done, cook for 10 more minutes.
11. Once it's done, take it out and let it get cool before serving.
12. Enjoy.

Serving Suggestion: Serve it with a dollar of the vanilla ice cream.

Variation Tip: Use dairy milk instead of almond milk.

Nutritional Information Per Serving: Calories 760| Fat43.3 g| Sodium644 mg | Carbs 93.2g | Fiber5.3 g | Sugar 70.2g | Protein 6.2g

Chapter 9-4 Weeks Diet Plan

Week-1

Day-1
Breakfast: Pumpkin Muffins
Lunch: Salmon Nuggets
Snack: Onion Rings
Dinner: Air Fryer Meatloaves
Dessert: Zesty Cranberry Scones

Day-2
Breakfast: Cinnamon Toasts
Lunch: Breaded Scallops
Snack: Strawberries and Walnuts Muffins
Dinner: Crumbed Chicken Katsu
Dessert: Apple Nutmeg Flautas

Day-3
Breakfast: Sweet Potatoes Hash
Lunch: Ham Burger Patties
Snack: Peppered Asparagus
Dinner: Crusted Chicken Breast
Dessert: Oreo Rolls

Day-4
Breakfast: Bacon and Egg Omelet
Lunch: Seafood Shrimp Omelet
Snack: Spicy Chicken Tenders
Dinner: Lamb Shank with Mushroom Sauce
Dessert: Lemon Sweet Twists

Day-5
Breakfast: Spinach Egg Muffins
Lunch: Curly Fries
Snack: Fried Halloumi Cheese
Dinner: Salmon with Green Beans
Dessert: Fudge Brownies

Day-6
Breakfast: Banana and Raisins Muffins
Lunch: Glazed Thighs with French Fries
Snack: Parmesan Crush Chicken
Dinner: Pork Chops
Dessert: Bread Pudding

Day-7
Breakfast: Morning Patties
Lunch: Wings with Corn on Cob
Snack: Potato Tater Tots
Dinner: Short Ribs & Root Vegetables
Dessert: Chocolate Chip Cake

Week-2

Day-1
Breakfast: Breakfast Casserole
Lunch: Sweet Potatoes with Honey Butter
Snack: Cheddar Quiche
Dinner: Zucchini Pork Skewers
Dessert: Mini Blueberry Pies

Day-2
Breakfast: Crispy Hash Browns
Lunch: Spicy Fish Fillet with Onion Rings
Snack: Crispy Plantain Chips
Dinner: Chicken Potatoes
Dessert: Apple Hand Pies

Day-3
Breakfast: Egg with Baby Spinach
Lunch: Zucchini Cakes
Snack: Blueberries Muffins
Dinner: Glazed Steak Recipe
Dessert: Mini Strawberry and Cream Pies

Day-4
Breakfast: Biscuit Balls
Lunch: Salmon Patties
Snack: Chicken Crescent Wraps
Dinner: Chicken Drumettes
Dessert: Chocolate Chip Cake

Day-5
Breakfast: Egg and Avocado in The Ninja Foodi
Lunch: Beef Cheeseburgers
Snack: Stuffed Bell Peppers
Dinner: Pork Chops with Broccoli
Dessert: Apple Nutmeg Flautas

Day-6
Breakfast: Breakfast Bacon
Lunch: Green Beans with Baked Potatoes
Snack: Chicken Stuffed Mushrooms
Dinner: Chicken Thighs with Brussels sprouts
Dessert: Fudge Brownies

Day-7
Breakfast: Breakfast Sausage Omelet
Lunch: Frozen Breaded Fish Fillet
Snack: Sweet Bites
Dinner: Steak in Air Fry
Dessert: Air Fried Bananas

Week-3

Day-1
Breakfast: Pepper Egg Cups
Lunch: Salmon with Fennel Salad
Snack: Parmesan French Fries
Dinner: Bang-Bang Chicken
Dessert: Tasty Pumpkin Muffins

Day-2
Breakfast: Bacon and Eggs for Breakfast
Lunch: Scallops with Greens
Snack: Dijon Cheese Sandwich
Dinner: Chicken Leg Piece
Dessert: Zesty Cranberry Scones

Day-3
Breakfast: Morning Egg Rolls
Lunch: Buttered Mahi-Mahi
Snack: Crispy Tortilla Chips
Dinner: Turkey and Beef Meatballs
Dessert: Bread Pudding

Day-4
Breakfast: Sausage with Eggs
Lunch: Balsamic Duck Breast
Snack: Grill Cheese Sandwich
Dinner: Lime Glazed Tofu
Dessert: Oreo Rolls

Day-5
Breakfast: Air Fried Sausage
Lunch: Garlic Herbed Baked Potatoes
Snack: Cauliflower Gnocchi
Dinner: Pork Chops with Brussels Sprouts
Dessert: Mini Blueberry Pies

Day-6
Breakfast: Yellow Potatoes with Eggs
Lunch: Beef & Broccoli
Snack: Chicken Tenders
Dinner: Spicy Chicken
Dessert: Biscuit Doughnuts

Day-7
Breakfast: Sweet Potatoes Hash
Lunch: Fresh Mix Veggies in Air Fryer
Snack: Chicken Crescent Wraps
Dinner: Cornish Hen with Baked Potatoes
Dessert: Chocolate Chip Muffins

Week-4

Day-1
Breakfast: Crispy Hash Browns
Lunch: Kale and Spinach Chips
Snack: Onion Rings
Dinner: Beer Battered Fish Fillet
Dessert: Walnuts Fritters

Day-2
Breakfast: Bacon and Egg Omelet
Lunch: Pickled Chicken Fillets
Snack: Sweet Bites
Dinner: Crispy Catfish
Dessert: Lemony Sweet Twists

Day-3
Breakfast: Morning Patties
Lunch: Two-Way Salmon
Snack: Cheddar Quiche
Dinner: Crusted Tilapia
Dessert: Apple Crisp

Day-4
Breakfast: Yellow Potatoes with Eggs
Lunch: Air Fried Turkey Breast
Snack: Dijon Cheese Sandwich
Dinner: Salmon with Broccoli and Cheese
Dessert: Air Fryer Sweet Twists

Day-5
Breakfast: Bacon and Eggs for Breakfast
Lunch: Chicken Wings
Snack: Strawberries and Walnuts Muffins
Dinner: Yogurt Lamb Chops
Dessert: Air Fried Beignets

Day-6
Breakfast: Air Fried Sausage
Lunch: Bell Peppers with Sausages
Snack: Crispy Tortilla Chips
Dinner: Lemon Pepper Salmon with Asparagus
Dessert: Cake in the Air Fryer

Day-7
Breakfast: Cinnamon Toasts
Lunch: Quinoa Patties
Snack: Potato Tater Tots
Dinner: General Tso's Chicken
Dessert: Apple Hand Pies

Conclusion

If you plan to buy the Ninja Air Fryer Max XL, then this cookbook is a perfect choice. It has seven cooking functions. I hope you will understand all the cooking functions and operating buttons of this appliance. I added recipes in this book; you can prepare food with this appliance. You didn't need to buy a separate oven or dehydrator to bake or dehydrate food. This appliance offers all the useful functions that you need. This cooking function has a large capacity. You can prepare food for a large family. Thank you for choosing my book!

Appendix Measurement Conversion Chart

VOLUME EQUIVALENTS(DRY)

US STANDARD	METRIC (APPROXIMATE)
1/8 teaspoon	0.5 mL
1/4 teaspoon	1 mL
1/2 teaspoon	2 mL
3/4 teaspoon	4 mL
1 teaspoon	5 mL
1 tablespoon	15 mL
1/4 cup	59 mL
1/2 cup	118 mL
3/4 cup	177 mL
1 cup	235 mL
2 cups	475 mL
3 cups	700 mL
4 cups	1 L

VOLUME EQUIVALENTS(LIQUID)

US STANDARD	US STANDARD (OUNCES)	METRIC (APPROXIMATE)
2 tablespoons	1 fl.oz.	30 mL
1/4 cup	2 fl.oz.	60 mL
1/2 cup	4 fl.oz.	120 mL
1 cup	8 fl.oz.	240 mL
1 1/2 cup	12 fl.oz.	355 mL
2 cups or 1 pint	16 fl.oz.	475 mL
4 cups or 1 quart	32 fl.oz.	1 L
1 gallon	128 fl.oz.	4 L

TEMPERATURES EQUIVALENTS

FAHRENHEIT(F)	CELSIUS(C) (APPROXIMATE)
225 °F	107 °C
250 °F	120 °C
275 °F	135 °C
300 °F	150 °C
325 °F	160 °C
350 °F	180 °C
375 °F	190 °C
400 °F	205 °C
425 °F	220 °C
450 °F	235 °C
475 °F	245 °C
500 °F	260 °C

WEIGHT EQUIVALENTS

US STANDARD	METRIC (APPROXIMATE)
1 ounce	28 g
2 ounces	57 g
5 ounces	142 g
10 ounces	284 g
15 ounces	425 g
16 ounces (1 pound)	455 g
1.5 pounds	680 g
2 pounds	907 g

© Copyright 2021 – All rights reserved

This document is geared towards providing exact and reliable information with regards to the topic and issue covered. The publication is sold with the idea that the publisher is not required to render accounting, officially permitted, or otherwise, qualified services. If advice is necessary, legal, or professional, a practiced individual in the profession should be ordered. - From a Declaration of Principles which was accepted and approved equally by a Committee of the American Bar Association and a Committee of Publishers and Associations. In no way is it legal to reproduce, duplicate, or transmit any part of this document in either electronic means or in printed format. Recording of this publication is strictly prohibited and any storage of this document is not allowed unless with written permission from the publisher.

All rights reserved. The information provided herein is stated to be truthful and consistent, in that any liability, in terms of inattention or otherwise, by any usage or abuse of any policies, processes, or directions contained within is the solitary and utter responsibility of the recipient reader.

Under no circumstances will any legal responsibility or blame be held against the publisher for any reparation, damages, or monetary loss due to the information herein, either directly or indirectly. Respective authors own all copyrights not held by the publisher.

The information herein is offered for informational purposes solely, and is universal as

so. The presentation of the information is without contract or any type of guarantee assurance. The trademarks that are used are without any consent, and the publication of the trademark is without permission or backing by the trademark owner.

All trademarks and brands within this book are for clarifying purposes only and are the owned by the owners themselves, not affiliated with this document.

Made in the USA
Monee, IL
15 December 2022

21871949R00058